SAT Grammar - Yellow

Homework: Version 1.3

Table of Contents

Yellow Grammar 1

Introduction to the Writing Section of the SAT

In 2005, the College Board created the writing section of the Scholastic Aptitude Test. This section was created to test students' understanding of grammar and to evaluate their ability to write clearly. It counts for a third of your SAT score, so it's certainly nothing to dismiss. In this lesson, we will discuss the three types of questions in the writing section of the test.

Identifying Sentence Errors

These questions present a sentence in which there is a possible error. Four different parts of the sentence are underlined, and usually one of the underlined sections is in error. There is also a fifth part for no error. Take a look below:

A person <u>who is</u> always chasing after <u>their</u> dreams <u>is bound</u> to be disappointed <u>in the end</u>.   <u>No Error</u>
      A   B   C   D   E

One of the underlined sections has an error. If you fixed that underlined section, the sentence would be correct. Can you tell which part is wrong?

("A person" is a singular subject; you can't use the plural possessive pronoun "their" to refer to "a person." The answer is B.)

Identifying Sentence Error questions tend to test students on topics such as subject-verb agreement, pronoun errors, adjective/adverb confusion , and verb tenses. Take a look at the following five questions and answer them to the best of your ability.

1. John <u>didn't know</u> that <u>the phone</u> had already <u>rang</u> ten times before he <u>picked it up</u>.   <u>No Error</u>
           A   B   C   D   E

2. The school <u>is reluctant</u> to <u>release</u> its <u>confidential</u> records to <u>Frank and I</u>. <u>No Error</u>
                 A   B   C   D   E

3. I <u>think that</u> the number of car accidents <u>rises</u> <u>every time</u> it snows <u>around here</u>. <u>No Error</u>
      A   B   C   D   E

4. Visitors <u>to</u> the <u>national history center</u> should <u>attach</u> a visitor badge to <u>his</u> chest. <u>No Error</u>
        A   B   C   D   E

5. The <u>thieves' heist</u> was <u>careful</u> planned, but the robbers <u>were foiled</u> by a security guard <u>who had</u>
        A   B   C   D

stayed late. <u>No Error</u>
              E

Don't be afraid to pick "no error"; about one in five questions is correct as it is written. (Just like one out of the five above is E!)

Improving Sentences

The second section of the writing portion of the SAT is the Improving Sentences section. It tests your knowledge of how sentences are put together.   Each question will give you a sentence with a section underlined. . Occasionally, the entire sentence will be underlined. In either case, the underlined portion will usually contain an error. Below the sentence there will be five answer choices, each showing a way to fix the error.

<u>To say that she is smart is like</u> saying Bill Gates is rich.

    A) To say that she is smart is like

    B) Saying that she is smart is similar in regards to

    C) If one were to say she was smart, like

    D) Saying she is smart is like

    E) To say she is smart, one could compare her by

As you can see, choice (A) is the same as the original sentence; picking (A) means "no error." (Like the "identifying sentence errors" section, about 20% of improving sentences questions are correct as written.) So what's wrong with this one? We're comparing two things ("she" being smart, and Bill Gates being rich) but the verb structure of the first part ("to say she is smart…") is different than that of the second part ("saying Bill Gates is rich"). It would sound better if they were similar: "Saying she is smart is like saying Bill Gates is rich." That narrows things down to (B) and (D), and (B) is just a bit too wordy. So our answer is (D).

Version 1.3

Improving Sentences questions test your knowledge of concepts such as sentence fragments, run-on sentences or comma splices, misplaced modifiers, faulty parallelism, sentence coordination/subordination, and wordiness. There are a few questions about verb tenses and pronoun usage, but in general Improving Sentences questions test your ability to construct a sentence. Try these three questions:

1. Determined to win the gold medal, <u>Jonathan's workout regime included</u> sprints, pushups, sit-ups, and endurance tests.

   A) Jonathan's workout regime included

   B) Jonathan had a regime, that worked him out with

   C) Jonathan devised a workout regime that included

   D) the workout Jonathan included

   E) Jonathan included a workout with

2. Because the roads are so slick from the snow, <u>so you should drive slowly and carefully</u>.

   A) so you should drive slowly and carefully

   B) for that reason, you should drive slowly and carefully

   C) you should drive slowly and in a careful manner

   D) you should drive slowly and carefully.

   E) driving should be done slowly and carefully.

3. Some of the students were glad to have school uniforms, <u>but others in the school hating it.</u>

   A) but others in the school hating it

   B) however others in the school hated it

   C) others, hating it, were against the idea

   D) so others in the school hated it

   E) but other students hated it

Improving Paragraphs

The final section of the writing test is the Improving Paragraphs section. This section is often the smallest – with five or six questions – but it is not the quickest. This is because you will have a short essay to read and correct. The questions for this section ask how to improve the paragraphs you have read by combining sentences, rearranging the order of the sentences, or clarifying points. Ever edited a friend's paper, or your own? Think of the Improving Paragraphs section as a form of peer editing.

Take a look at the following excerpt and question:

(6) Many people throughout the city barricaded themselves in their homes, fearful of being attacked. (7) They waited for help from the police, the government, or anyone who could help. (8) The governor of the state sent in the National Guard to quell the riots. (9) Many people criticized this decision. (10) The wisdom of his decision was soon proved when the situation was resolved peacefully.

In context, what is the best way to combine Sentences 8 and 9 (recreated below)?

(8) The governor of the state sent in the National Guard to quell the riots. (9) Many people criticized this decision.

A) The governor of the state, sending in the National Guard to quell the riots and cause many people to criticize his decision.

B) Many people criticized the governor's decision to send in the National Guard in an attempt to quell riots.

C) Quelling the riots, the governor of the state earned much criticism by using the National Guard.

D) The governor of the state sent in the National Guard to quell the riots, a decision which was criticized by many people.

E) Criticized by many people, the governor's decision was to send in the National Guard to quell the riots.

The best way to combine the two sentences will make the sentence fit in well with the progress of ideas in the paragraph. Notice that sentence 7 mentions people waiting for help, and sentence 10 discusses the wisdom of the governor's decision to send in the National Guard. So it would make logical sense to combine sentences 8 and 9 so that the new sentence begins with help and ends with the governor's

decision. This rules out (B) and (E). (A) is a sentence fragment; the subject "governor" has no main verb. (C) implies that the governor himself quelled the riots; since it is unclear, we should rule it out. That leaves (D), which is grammatically correct and provides a transition from the first idea to the second.

Read the following paragraphs and answer the questions that follow.

(1) Lewis Carroll's classic <u>Alice in Wonderland</u> is celebrated the world over. (2) Both adults and children love the surreal adventures of the little girl who gets lost in another world. (3) Some people might ask "Why? Did Lewis Carroll write such a strange story?" (4) Indeed, many of the things Alice encounters and many of the stories she hears are nonsensical. (5) What did Carroll mean? (6) Does his story have a point?

(7) In fact, Carroll deliberately intended his writing to be silly. (8) Most children's tales from that time were written with lessons. (9) These stories were meant to give children moral improvement. (10) Carroll himself thought that children's literature shouldn't force lessons on children who just wanted to have fun. (11) Instead, he wrote stories that celebrated nonsense. (12) There are also some clever references to political figures and mathematical concepts that children would not be able to understand.

1. In context, which is the best way to rewrite sentence 3?

   A. Some people asking "Why did Lewis Carroll write such a strange story?"

   B. Despite its popularity, some people wonder why Lewis Carroll wrote such a strange story.

   C. Why was Lewis Carroll's story so strange, was what many people wondered.

   D. Some people might ask "why Lewis Carroll wrote such a strange story"?

   E. Why did Lewis Carroll, so popular with all, write such a strange story?

2. What is the best way to combine sentences 8 and 9?

    A. Most children's tales from that time were written with lessons, they were meant to improve children's morals.

    B. Written to improve children's morals, most children's tales had lessons.

    C. Most children's tales from that time were written with lessons in order to improve children's moral behavior.

    D. Improving morals was the main focus of children's tales from that time, which were written with lessons.

    E. Children's tales, written with lessons, were intended to morally improve children of that time.

3. Which of the following revisions would most improve the overall coherence of the essay?

    A. Move sentence 7 to the beginning of Paragraph 1

    B. Switch the order of sentences 4 and 5

    C. Move sentence 12 before sentence 5.

    D. Delete sentence 12.

    E. Delete sentence 2.

HOMEWORK

1. Name three grammatical errors that are tested by the Identifying Sentence Errors section:

    1) plural possessive pronoun
    2) singular subject
    3) subject-verb agreement

2. Name three grammatical errors that are tested by the Improving Sentences section:

    1) Sentence fragments
    2) run-on sentences
    3) comma splices

3. Name two things the Improving Paragraphs section might ask you to do:

    1)

    2)

Write 2 examples of an identifying sentence errors question:

1) _____

   _____

   _____(E) No Error

2) _____

   _____

   _____(E) No Error

On the lines below, write an example of an improving sentences question.

Q: _____

_____

_____

A) _____

B) _____

C) _____

D) _____

E) _____

Yellow Grammar 2

Sentence Structure

Parts of the Sentence

Many of the questions on the SAT writing section will test your knowledge of how a sentence works. Consequently, it is wise to review the different parts of the sentence. Take a look at the following sentence:

> The young man studied math and reading.

Now let's break it down.

<u>The young man</u> – this is the **subject** of the sentence. The subject is the noun(s) or pronoun(s) that either performs the action of the verb or indicates the main idea of the sentence. In this case, the young man is performing the action of studying.

<u>Studied</u> – This is the **main verb** of the sentence, also known as the **predicate**. In essence, the verb tells what the subject DOES.

Every sentence – and every clause, independent or dependent – NEEDS A SUBJECT AND A VERB! Without a subject and a verb, a sentence is not complete.

<u>Math and reading</u> – this is the **direct object**. The direct object is the part of the sentence that receives the action of the verb. It answers the question "what" or "whom" after an action verb. The young man is studying what? He's studying math and science.

Exercise 1

Read the sentences below and underline the subject, circle the verb, and draw a box around the direct object, if there is one.

1. Packs of wild dogs roam the city at night.
2. Famed explorer Lance Reynolds has just returned from his travels in the Arctic.
3. For Christmas, Paul prepared the turkey.
4. The focus on science in this school has improved students' grades.
5. I bought three albums today.

Types of Sentences

Unfortunately, not all sentences are as simple as the ones we just discussed. Look at the sentence below:

> Paul tried to cook a difficult meal, but he was disappointed when his soufflé collapsed in the oven.

There are three subjects! Three predicates! What to do? A quick review of the different *types* of sentences should help make things more clear.

SIMPLE

A simple sentence has just one subject and one predicate.

> Jean-Ralphio wears designer clothing all the time.

> Sheriff Albertson will be here shortly.

Sometimes, a simple sentence is just one part of a larger sentence. When a simple sentence is part of a larger sentence, it is called an **independent clause**. A clause is a section of a sentence. An independent clause can stand by itself. Another type of clause – a **dependent clause**, cannot stand alone. All clauses must have a subject and a predicate.

COMPOUND

A compound sentence has two independent clauses, connected by either a semicolon (;) or a comma and a **coordinating conjunction**. (The best way to remember all the coordinating conjunctions is the acronym FANBOYS – for, and, nor, but, or, yet, so.)

> I am a teacher**, and** my wife is a doctor.

> Abed tried to get chicken fingers at the cafeteria**, but** he was too late.

> I did not like that movie**;** it had too much violence.

COMPLEX

Complex sentences have an independent clause and a **dependent clause**. Remember: A dependent clause cannot stand by itself, but like an independent clause, a dependent clause has both a subject and a verb.

> Mark was not able to go on the field trip **because he did not have a permission slip.**

In the above sentence, "because he did not have a permission slip" is the dependent clause. Note the subject ("he") and the predicate ("did not have"). Note, too, that the clause cannot stand by itself as a sentence.

A **subordinating** conjunction connects a dependent clause to an independent clause. In this case, "because" is the subordinating conjunction; it makes the dependent clause dependent. Other examples of subordinating conjunctions are *after, although, before, if, since, than, that, though, unless, until, when, whenever, where, wherever, whether,* and *while*. You do not need to memorize this list

Unauthorized copying or reuse of any part of this page is illegal.

Version 1.3

to figure out if a clause is dependent or independent; just try to determine whether the clause could stand by itself. If the clause can stand alone, it is independent. If it cannot stand alone, it is dependent. Using any of the subordinating conjunctions will assure that the clause cannot stand alone.

COMPOUND-COMPLEX

A compound-complex sentence has at least one dependent clause and at least two independent clauses.

> When they told me about the fight, I was upset, but I didn't let it show.

This is like the first sentence we saw at the beginning of this section; three subjects, three verbs. The first clause, "When they told me about the fight," is dependent. The next two clauses ("I was upset, but I didn't let it show.") are independent clauses, connected by a coordinating conjunction.

Exercise 2

Read the sentences below. Underline the independent clauses, circle dependent clauses, and identify the type of sentence on the line below.

1. Whenever we go to the dog park, Barkley begs and pleads to be let off his leash.

   _____

2. Pete's favorite hobby is collecting Transformers toys.

   _____

3. The famous company is going to go bankrupt if the designers don't come up with a new concept.

   _____

4. Sharks do not want to eat humans; they usually prefer seals or small fish.

   _____

5. Lando did not want to betray Han, but he was forced to turn his friend over to the Empire when Darth Vader changed the rules of their agreement.

   _____

HOMEWORK

Write two examples of simple sentences.

1. I will be at your house shortly.
2. Becca always wears white clothes.

Write two examples of compound sentences.

1. I love to study my math work, but I fancy Reading alot more.

2. Allen like the film, but I didnot, it was too loud.

Write three examples of complex sentences.

1. Sarah was out picking flowers while Rachel was cutting bread.

2. We need to buy our tickets for the movies before we get our drinks.

3. I will need to pay for my ticket unless he decides to get it for me.

Write three examples of compound-complex sentences.

1. my dad made me very angry, so I hit him, but I felt bad after.

2. I wore black because I thought it would be cold, but it was hot, so I changed.

3. She always had her nails painted red, but they were blue today, I was suprised on the change she made.

Look at the questions below. One out of the four sentences is incorrect. Circle the incorrect sentence.

1.   A) Frank and Maddy went to the fair.

        B) When Frank and Maddy went to the fair, they bought popcorn.

        C) They rode each of the rides they had so much fun.

        D) It was a wonderful time for both of them.

2.   A) While you buy the turkey, I will prepare the stuffing.

        B) Ethan will make the cranberry sauce.

        C) Everyone worked in the kitchen for hours, and we couldn't wait to eat.

        D) When the clock struck six, and everyone sat down to eat Thanksgiving dinner.

3.   A) I told Vidhi to be back by six, but when I looked for her she was nowhere to be found.

        B) Her mother was beside herself with worry; so we called Vidhi's friends.

        C) None of them knew where she could be, and Vidhi's mother began to cry.

        D) What a surprise it was when Vidhi walked in the back door; she had been in the back yard!

4.   A) My favorite rock group is the Blithering Idiots.

        B) They formed in 2001 when Angus Thorplemaple put an ad in the paper for a drummer and a guitarist.

        C) Their first big hit, "I Found It on Top of the Fridge," debuted in 2002.

        D) They continued touring; until they ran out of money.

HOMEWORK – Subject/Verb Agreement Preview

Directions: Correct the error in each sentence. If there is none, write "no error."

1. The performance of the much-anticipated new model G cars ~~have~~ *had* met with mixed reviews from buyers and auto specialists alike.

   _____

   _____

2. Not a single case of bubonic plague or bacterial meningitis ~~have~~ *had* been reported here for decades.

   _____

   _____

3. The decision to abandon the project and devote resources to other endeavors ~~have~~ *has* been severely criticized by many within the organization.

   _____

   _____

4. Among the archaeologist's findings ~~were~~ *was* a mysterious pyramidal structure that is thought to pre date the arrival of Slavic peoples to the region.

   _____

   _____

5. The primary component of the new laws allow students to transfer out of schools that have been deemed "in-need-of-improvement".

   _____

   _____

6. Michael "Beachball" Jacobite, along with his teammates "Sandy" Sam Willis and "Carrot-Top" Ka bob, has finally decided to retire from the sport of beach volleyball.

   have

   _____

   _____

7. The central measures of the Kyoto Protocol and its accompanying legislation concerns the reduction of greenhouse gases.

   _____

   _____

8. Despite all the efforts to preserve and protect farmland, there remains but three known private farmsteads in the entire county.

   _____

   _____

9. The location of the new office buildings and retail stores signal a desire to keep development contained within a few miles of downtown.

   _____

   _____

10. Neither the commissioner nor any of his chief aides have yet commented on Major League Baseball's new drug policies.

    _____

    _____

11. The film Girl with a Pearl Earring depicts the life of a young servant girl whose stunning beauty and otherworldly charm catches the fancy of the painter Vermeer.

    _____

    _____

12. The Western Pennsylvania Conservancy, along with many other regional environmental protection groups, hope to stem the tide of development around urbanized areas.

_____

_____

13. Each of the recent measures designed to root out organized crime and corruption have failed miserably.

_____

_____

14. The current team, which consists of both "homegrown" talent and proven veteran players, have the potential to reach the World Series.

_____

_____

15. Every one of the clown's silly gestures and comments get the audience laughing almost uncontrollably.

_____

_____

16. The issue of the effects of globalization on local cultures have inspired numerous books, articles, and even films over the last ten to fifteen years.

_____

_____

17. In the forested region of the country, on the opposite bank of the river, lurks a ferocious pack of wolves.

_____

_____

Unauthorized copying or reuse of any part of this page is illegal.

Version 1.3

18. To overcome one's harmful habits and addictions usually takes ~~one~~ a tremendous amount of courage and determination.

_____

_____

19. A decade of oppression and persecution in Sudan ~~have~~ *has* not been enough for the international community to take any significant action to help that country.

_____

_____

20. Neither of the two contestants have met the criteria to advance to the next round of the competition. *advancing*

_____

_____

Yellow Grammar 3

Fragments, Run-Ons, and Comma Splices

In the last lesson, we discussed the composition of sentences – how they're created from different parts of the sentence (clauses) and how those clauses are made up of different types of words. Several questions on the SAT writing section will deal with sentences that are written poorly – either they have too much in them, or too little.

Sentence Fragments

A sentence fragment is a sentence that is incomplete. It's missing something –such as a subject or a verb – that will make it a fully functioning sentence.

> **WRONG**: The proposal, sponsored by the senator from Kentucky.

All we have here is a subject! ("Sponsored," though it comes from the verb "sponsor," is being used here as an adjective describing the proposal.)

> **RIGHT**: The proposal is sponsored by the senator from Kentucky.

or

> **RIGHT**: The proposal, sponsored by the senator from Kentucky, has met with resistance.

A sentence fragment can also be missing a subject:

> **WRONG**: Having studied math for seven hours without a single break.

> **RIGHT**: Having studied math for seven hours without a single break, John was exhausted.

or

> **RIGHT**: John had studied math for seven hours without a single break.

Imperative sentences (sentences that make a request or give a command) may seem to be fragments, but they have an unstated subject: you.

> Go get the groceries from the car.
>
> Empty the dishwasher before you go.
>
> Buy these wonderful magic beans!

Even in compound, complex, and compound-complex sentences, clauses might be missing subjects or predicates. The longer the sentence, the more difficult it is to spot a fragment.

> **WRONG**: Because it is well known for its libraries which hold documents thousands of years old, the city of Timbuktu often known as "the black pearl of the desert."
>
> **RIGHT**: Because it is well known for its libraries which hold documents thousands of years old, the city of Timbuktu **is** often known as "the black pearl of the desert."

Occasionally, you may come across a dependent clause by itself. This also counts as a fragment.

> **WRONG**: Since Charles had lost most of his money at the casino.
>
> **RIGHT**: Since Charles had lost most of his money at the casino, he couldn't pay his rent.

Read each sentence below and determine if it is complete or a fragment. If the sentence is a fragment, write under the sentence whether it is missing a subject or a predicate.

Exercise 1

1. Antwon searching for a new videogame to play.

2. All smoking in the building will be prohibited after January 1st.

3. Purchased by the financiers who recently made a killing on the stock market.

4. Lebron James, who is considered one of today's top athletes.

5. Major Burns does not approve of Captain Pierce's shenanigans.

6. Cooler, drier air arriving this morning, and rain showers possible this evening.

Run-On Sentences

The other common sentence error involves cramming too much in a sentence.

Brian was always late for school he needed to buy a bike.

These two ideas ("Brian needed to buy a bike" and "he was always late to school") are related; one can assume that if Brian buys a bike, he won't be late to school any more. They are also both independent clauses – each idea could stand by itself as a whole sentence. However, you can't just smoosh those two ideas together without something to separate them.

WRONG: Brian was always late to school, he needed to buy a bike.

A comma does NOT connect two independent clauses. This is a common error called a **comma splice**. While commas can separate different types of clauses, they do not connect two independent clauses. Well, how to fix it? You can connect two independent clauses with a semicolon:

RIGHT: Brian was always late for school; he needed to buy a bike.

Or you could split the sentence entirely:

RIGHT: Brian was always late for school. He needed to buy a bike.

Another possibility is to use a **coordinating conjunction** (such as *and, or, but, so,* and *yet*) to connect the two ideas:

RIGHT: Brian was always late for school, **so** he needed to buy a bike.

Yet another option is to turn one of the independent clauses into a dependent clause by using a subordinating conjunction:

RIGHT: Brian needed to buy a bike **because** he was always late for school.

A warning: conjunctive adverbs, such as *however, meanwhile, accordingly,* and *therefore*, are NOT conjunctions. They cannot connect two independent clauses. They can be used to establish a relationship between two independent clauses, if the clauses are separated by a semicolon.

WRONG: Brian thought the bike would be expensive, however, it was much cheaper than he expected.

RIGHT: Brian thought the bike would be expensive**;** however, it was much cheaper than he expected.

Exercise 2

Read the sentences below. Determine if they are run-on sentences or if they are correct as written. If you find that a sentence is incorrect, and then rewrite it in one of the ways discussed above.

1. Because the trade agreement guarantees new jobs, financial analysts predict an upturn for the economy, they are very hopeful.

_____

_____

2. Paul is awfully proud of his expensive pool table, however, he is a terrible pool player.

_____

_____

3. When word spread that the catered food had gone bad, the angry bride and groom demanded a refund.

_____

_____

4. Cats are extremely clean creatures, they groom themselves with their tongues.

_____

_____

5. I can't believe Andrew won the hot-dog eating contest, he's so skinny!

_____

_____

PRACTICE

Try out these Improving Sentences questions.

Run-On Sentences:

1. Hockney's most arresting work has been produced at his home in <u>Los Angeles, he moved there</u> from his native Britain.

   (A) Los Angeles, he moved there

   (B) Los Angeles; he moved there

   (C) Los Angeles, but he moved there

(D) Los Angeles and he moved there

(E) Los Angeles he moved there

2. Banquets are frequently thrown to honor guests in a Chinese <u>home, they often feature</u> shark fin as the main dish.

   (A) home, they often feature

   (B) home; often feature

   (C) home and often feature

   (D) home and they often feature

   (E) home, these often feature

3. <u>Many well-heeled taxpayers pay</u> less than 10 percent of their annual income to the Internal Revenue Service, some middle-income taxpayers pay a much larger percentage annually.

   (A) Many well-heeled taxpayers pay

   (B) However, many well-heeled taxpayers pay

   (C) With many well-heeled taxpayers which pay

   (D) Many a well-heeled taxpayer pays

   (E) Although many well-heeled taxpayers pay

4. Most western European countries have decreased their consumption of fossil <u>fuels, a number of eastern European countries, however, have</u> not done so.

   (A) fuels, a number of eastern European countries, however, have

   (B) fuels, however a number of eastern European countries have

   (C) fuels, while on the other hand a number of eastern European countries have

   (D) fuels; a number of eastern European countries, however, have

   (E) fuels, a number however of eastern European countries have

Sentence Fragments:

1. It would appear that no significant portion of the electorate <u>troubled by doubts</u> substantial enough to result in the defeat of the incumbent.

   (A) troubled by doubts

   (B) is troubled by doubts

   (C) troubled by doubts which are

   (D) are troubled with doubts, these are

   (E) being troubled with doubts that are

2. Most students enter college right after high school, <u>while a few waiting a year or two before seeking admission</u>.

   (A) while a few waiting a year or two before seeking admission

   (B) and a few, waiting a year or two before seeking admission

   (C) but a few wait a year or two before seeking admission

   (D) but a wait of a year or two is sought by a few

   (E) though a few will have begun to wait a year or two before seeking admission

3. Mysteriously beautiful, the Nepalese shrine <u>inlaid with semiprecious stones</u> rare enough to honor the spiritual essence of the Buddha.

   (A) inlaid with semiprecious stones

   (B) inlaid with semiprecious stones which are

   (C) being inlaid with semiprecious stones that are

   (D) is inlaid with semiprecious stones

   (E) is inlaid with semiprecious stones, these are

4. The general increase in salaries <u>surprised and delighted the employees</u>.

   (A) surprised and delighted the employees

   (B) surprised the employees, delighting them

   (C) surprised the employees and they were delighted

   (D) was a surprise and caused delight among the employees

   (E) was surprising to the employees, delighting them

5. For reasons not fully understood, nearly all children on the island <u>gifted with musical ability</u> so strong they can master any instrument within hours

   (A) gifted with musical ability

   (B) gifted with musical ability which is

   (C) are gifted with musical ability

   (D) being gifted with musical ability that is

   (E) are gifted with musical abilities, these are

6. <u>That many people believe him to be</u> the most competent and well-informed of all the candidates currently listed on the ballot.

   (A) That many people believe him to be

   (B) That many people believe he is

   (C) Because many people believe him to be

   (D) Many people believe him to be

   (E) That many people believe him

HOMEWORK:

Write two examples of sentence fragments.

1. _____

2. _____

Now write complete versions of those fragments.

1. _____

2. _____

Write two examples of run-on sentences.

1. _____
   _____

2. _____
   _____

Write corrected versions of those run-on sentences.

1. _____
   _____

2. _____
   _____

Directions: Correct the error in each sentence. If there is none, write "no error."

1. Word spread that the dam had broken, then the residents of Smallville fled from their homes and ran east to higher ground.

_____

_____

2. A small fraction of the populace, convinced that the Prime Minister and his cohorts were plotting to lead the country to war and eliminate the current system of social benefits.

_____

_____

3. The man assumed that the knocking on the door was merely that of a "late visitor," nevertheless, he was a bit apprehensive.

_____

_____

4. The New York City subway system is notorious for its giant rats, a few of these have been known to weigh as much as thirty pounds.

_____

_____

5. The killing of humpback whales was made illegal in the 1980s; today, however, a couple of Nordic and north Asian countries, preparing to reinstitute the practice.

_____

_____

6. Their rejection of several key provisions of the treaty, which had been drawn up by the Security Council and approved by the General Assembly.

_____

_____

7. The man seemed despondent about his life as a lowly shoemaker, however, he performed his job with gusto and skill.

_____

_____

8. Coverage of international news, too often neglected in favor of other, seemingly less urgent concerns such as the court trials of famous celebrities and the latest reality TV scandal.

_____

_____

9. For centuries popes were chosen from among the ranks of Italian cardinals, this practice seems, however, to have ended.

_____

_____

10. Having been forced into retirement because of his association with a group of men found to be plotting to assassinate the supreme leader and create anarchy throughout the country.

_____

_____

11. Although rejected by the journal's review board twice, the group's article could, with some emendations and additional data, ultimately be accepted for publication.

_____

_____

12. In 1906 Chicago ruled the baseball world; both of its teams, the Cubs and the White Sox, competing against each other in the World Series that year.

_____

_____

13. Senator Howard's opposition to capital punishment is well-known, yet he has not signed the current proposal to outlaw the death penalty nationwide.

_____

_____

14. The new film <u>Water</u>, which depicts the hardships faced by a group of widows who have been cast out of their families and forced to live in miserable conditions.

_____

_____

15. Several leading scientists who have recently published a paper that purports to show a genetic link between the ancient Phoenicians and the modern-day Lebanese.

_____

_____

16. For almost an entire year, from the summer of 1940 to June of 1941, Great Britain stood virtually alone against the Nazi onslaught, vulnerable and weakened, but determined to survive.

_____

_____

17. The fugitives fled across the Canadian border and fell out of sight, while in Canada, they managed to elude capture for fifteen years.

_____

_____

18. Everybody in the gambling world suspected that the upcoming race had been "fixed"; yet, not knowing who had arranged the deal or which horse would actually win.

_____

_____

19. The English national team has not won the World Cup since 1966, that year was the miracle year that put England on the map as one of the world's elite soccer teams.

_____

_____

20. The sailors sleeping uneasily in their bunks when the alarm sounded and they were forced to man their stations and brace for the coming air attack.

_____

_____

Yellow Grammar 4

Verb Tense/Form

Introduction

When did it happen? Many questions on the SAT are concerned with this issue: whether verbs are being used in the correct tenses. (Tense, in case you've forgotten, is *when* the action described by the verb happens – whether it's in the present, the past, or the future.) On the SAT, you will be required to read many sentences and decide if the verbs they contain are written in the proper tense. Before you look at the possible answers, you should think about the sentence and consider the time frame that it describes. Ask yourself: is the action taking place in the past, present, or future? This will make it easier to narrow down your choices.

Here's an example.

Last week, Kevin <u>finishes</u> the race in nineteen minutes.

   a. finishes

   b. finished

   c. finish

   d. is finishing

In this case, the answer is B. The sentence says that the race was "last week", so we know the sentence should be in the *past tense* to show that the action already occurred.

A Quick Review of Types of Verbs

<u>Action verbs</u> tell what the subject does.

> Kevin **walked** the dog.

> Kevin **gave** his dog a bone.

<u>Linking verbs</u> link the subject to additional information about the subject.

> The dog **is** a Beagle.

> Her bark **sounds** friendly.

<u>Helping verbs</u> combine with the main verb to form a verb phrase.

> Kevin **will** walk the dog.

> The dog **can** walk two miles.

A Quick Review of Tenses

English has six tenses, and each has a simple form and a progressive form. You need to be familiar with the way each tense is used. This will help you to identify incorrect verb tenses while taking the SAT.

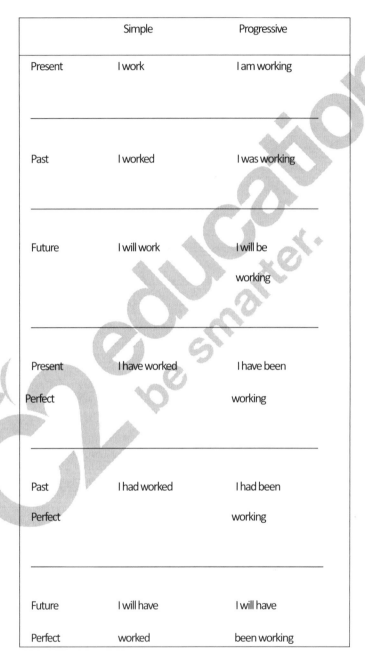

	Simple	Progressive
Present	I work	I am working
Past	I worked	I was working
Future	I will work	I will be working
Present Perfect	I have worked	I have been working
Past Perfect	I had worked	I had been working
Future Perfect	I will have worked	I will have been working

Note: All perfect tense verbs require <u>have, had, or has</u> before the main verb!

Version 1.3

Using the Present Tense

Use the present tense to describe a state or action occurring in the present time.

> Example: **I am** a student.

> Example: They **are studying** the Holy Roman Empire. (Use the present tense to describe habitual action.)

> Example: They **eat** at Joe's Diner every night.

> Example: My father never **drinks** coffee.

Use the present tense to describe things that are always true.

> Example: The earth **is** round.

> Example: Grass **is** green.

Exercise 1

Rewrite these following sentences using the present tense.

1. James broke the vase.

2. The car's engine did not start.

3. Patrique and Andrew will room together.

4. Jay and Gloria went on their honeymoon and had a great time.

5. The captain steered his ship between the dangerous icebergs.

Using the Past Tense

Use the simple past tense to describe an action or condition that took place or existed at a specific time in the past and is now over and done with.

> Example: Norman **broke** his toe when he tripped over his son's tricycle.

Exercise 2

Rewrite the following sentences in the past tense.

1. Elly shall visit her grandmother Tuesday.

2. Jarvis gives the flowers to Deborah.

3. The platypus smells something on the wind.

4. Emilia really looks forward to her favorite star's new movie.

5. Jennifer will dance with Patrick after the prom.

Using the Future Tense

Use the future tense for actions expected in the future. The future tense Is made by using either *will* or *shall* in front of the base form of the verb.

> Example: I **shall call** you on Wednesday.

> Example: The next president of the chess club **will need** to order new chess sets.

We often express future actions with the expression *to be going to*.

> Example: I **am going to move** to another apartment soon.

Exercise 3

Rewrite the following sentences in the future tense.

1. Paul went to the comic book store.

2. The next performer on the stage is famous children's entertainer Freddy Spaghetti.

3. My daughter Shauna attends Pickney Park Elementary School.

4. That new show about detectives in Mumbai is my favorite.

5. Eating asparagus and Brussels sprouts improves your digestion.

Using the Present Perfect Tense

Use the present perfect tense for actions and conditions that started in the past and continue up to and into the present time.

> Example: I **have been living** here for the last two years.

Use the present perfect for actions and conditions that happened a number of times in the past and may happen again in the future.

> Example: I **have heard** that song several times on the radio.

Use the present perfect for something that happened at an unspecified time in the past.

> Example: Anna **has seen** that movie already.

Using the Past Perfect Tense

The past perfect tense is used to represent past actions or conditions that were completed before other past actions or conditions. The more recent past event is expressed in the simple past, and the earlier past event is expressed in the past perfect.

> Example: When I turned my computer on this morning, I realized that I **had exited** the program yesterday without saving my work.

Using the Future Perfect Tense

Use the future perfect tense for a future state or event that will take place before another future event.

Example: By the end of the week, I **will have worked** four hours of overtime.

Exercise 4

Read the sentences below and identify which perfect tense is being used.

1. Alison has always been a big fan of grunge rock.

2. Roberto realized that he had locked himself out of his car.

3. By 2013, I will have lived in Florida for ten years.

4. We have never been back to that amusement park since our last visit.

5. Before we left for school, we had fed the cats and both dogs.

Exercise 5: Verb Tense Complete Review

Directions: Correct the error in each sentence. If there is none, write "no error."

1. When my father had finished washing the dishes, which had been lying in a heap in the sink for days, he retires to the living room to read the paper.

_____

_____

2. In the 17th century, European nations scoured the globe for riches and have established colonial footholds in foreign lands.

_____

_____

3. Last year, after firing half the staff in a fit of rage, the boss has warned me never to show up late for work again.

_____

_____

4. Before the army fled to the coast, it had put up a stout defense against the invading foreign forces.

_____

_____

5. Once news of the American victory at the Battle of Saratoga spread, the French will have agreed to aid the British colonists' struggle for independence.

_____

_____

6. News of the Avian flu's outbreak caused widespread panic and fear that soon the pandemic would have engulfed the whole nation.

_____

_____

7. It is a generally accepted economic principle that when demand for a good rises the price increased too.

_____

_____

8. Until the Confederates lost the Battle of Antietam, the British would consider allying with the South and granting the rebellious states international legitimacy.

_____

_____

9. Last Thursday, to the dismay of every man, woman, and child who had ever made a sarcastic vow, pigs begin flying through the skies of northern Iowa.

_____

_____

10. Democracy would not replace dictatorship in the region until political dissent becomes accepted and basic human rights are respected.

_____

_____

Verb Form:

Using the Proper Past Participle

If you use the present, past, or future perfect tense, make sure that you use *the past participle* and not the simple past tense.

> WRONG: I have **swam** in that pool every day this week.

> RIGHT: I have **swum** in that pool every day this week.

Notice that the past participle of the verb *swim* is *swum* and not *swimmed*. Although many past participle verbs are created by adding –ed to a base verb or by doubling the final consonant of a base verb and then adding –ed, that's not the case with swim and certain other verbs. These **irregular verbs** follow their own rules.

Irregular Verbs

Irregular verbs have two different forms for simple past and past participle tenses. For many verbs, the two forms are the same, as in *we walked* (past) and *we had walked* (past perfect), but for many "irregular" verbs, they are different, as in *we ate* (past) and *we had eaten* (past perfect). You should know the irregular forms of common verbs. The following are some of the most common irregular verbs. Study these irregular verbs so that you will be able to identify mistakes on the SAT.

Base Form	Simple Past	Past Participle
arise	arose	arisen
become	became	become
begin	began	begun
blow	blew	blown
break	broke	broken
come	came	come
do	did	done
draw	drew	drawn
drink	drank	drunk
drive	drove	driven
eat	ate	eaten
fall	fell	fallen
fly	flew	flown
freeze	froze	frozen
give	gave	given
grow	grew	grown
know	knew	known
ride	rode	ridden
rise	rose	risen
run	ran	run
see	saw	seen
shake	shook	shaken
shrink	shrank	shrunk
sing	sang	sung
speak	spoke	spoken
take	took	taken
throw	threw	thrown

Exercise 6: Irregular Verbs

Directions: Complete the following sentences with the correct form of the verb.

1. We would have _____ (to ride) even further if we had had the time.

2. Until now, the issue hasn't _____ (to arise).

3. Before we won last week's game, we hadn't _____ (to beat) the Cougars in 10 years.

4. I would not have _____ (to drink) the punch if I had known that it had liquor in it.

5. We searched everywhere, but our friends had _____ (to go) out for the evening.

6. Had I never _____ (to know) about video games, I would have _____ (to get) perfect grades last semester.

7. At last night's concert, the band _____ (to sing) all of its greatest hits.

8. The Donnellys have _____ (to run) their corner store for over 20 years.

9. They had _____ (to speak) for so long that the other speakers didn't have time to finish their presentations.

10. I can't believe you put my wool sweater in the dryer and _____ (to shrink) it.

11. His batting average has really _____ (to sink) ever since his injury.

12. It seems as if the tulips _____ (to spring) out of the ground overnight.

13. We should have _____ (to take) that shortcut to work.

14. If we had jumped over that fence, the polar bear would have _____ (to tear) us to shreds.

15. I promise you that by next month I will have _____ (to write) the first 4 chapters of the book.

Exercise 7: Verb Form Complete Review

Directions: Correct errors and rewrite the sentences.

1. By the time the children had fallen asleep, their parents had began assembling the kids' Christmas presents in the garage.

_____

_____

2. Dehydrated from a long afternoon run, Bill drunk five and a half bottles of Gatorade before he took a shower to cool off.

_____

_____

3. Before they could reach Charleston Harbor, the Federal ships were caught in a violent storm and blown off course.

_____

_____

4. The 1920 World Series was just getting underway in Brooklyn when it was learned that several White Sox players had threw the previous year's Series.

_____

_____

5. Steven had trouble focusing in the library because the cell phone of the inconsiderate person next to him rung incessantly.

_____

_____

6. When the market became glutted with oil, the price per barrel sunk considerably.

_____

_____

7. The principal, having swore he would not take away any more student privileges, broke his promise when he removed the Coke machines from the student commons.

_____

_____

8. Ordinary moviegoers and critics alike are gushing over Harriet's new film, which they claim is one of the greatest they ever saw.

_____

_____

9. Thinking that they had spotted a shark, the lifeguards swum briskly back to shore.

_____

_____

10. Jim's father became extremely upset when he went to clean up the yard on Saturday and found the rake broke in half.

_____

_____

11. Before Knight scored the winning run, Boston pitcher Stanley had threw a wild pitch that allowed Mitchell to come home and score the tying run.

_____

_____

12. Problems have repeatedly arose in school districts throughout the country since the new No Child Left Behind laws were ratified by Congress in 2001.

_____

_____

13. The king, having chose to flee the country rather than face down the revolutionaries, forfeited any political capital he may have still possessed.

_____

_____

14. The officer had ridden right past them not knowing that they were the suspects whom the police were searching for.

_____

_____

15. The old woman had shrank considerably since I last saw her ten years ago, when she worked as a seamstress in Paris.

_____

_____

Homework: Verb Tenses

Exercise 1: Paragraph Tense

In what tense should this paragraph be written? Which word in the first sentence tells the reader whether this should be present, past, or future tense? Some of the underlined verbs are already in the correct tense and others are not. Rewrite the paragraph so that all of the verbs in the story are in the same correct tense.

A wonderful thing <u>happening</u> yesterday. My friend <u>called</u> and <u>invite</u> me to come to her house. As I <u>walks</u> the two blocks to her house, a bright light <u>flashed</u> overhead and a shiny round object <u>falls</u> through the air. It <u>landed</u> a few feet away from me, and I <u>hurries</u> over to look at it. It was <u>nestles</u> in lush green grass and looked like a magical apple. It had a brilliant red glow and it <u>sparkled</u> and <u>flashing</u>. Then, as I <u>watching</u>, it <u>open</u> up! Inside <u>were</u> a beautiful fairy.

_____

_____

_____

_____

_____

Exercise 2

Directions: Correct the error in each sentence.

1. Tomorrow I go to the market.

_____

2. Yesterday I learn how to knit.

_____

3. This package didn't came with directions.

_____

4. There are ketchup and mustard in the refrigerator.

_____

5. She have knowledge and understanding about the topic.

_____

6. Are you always prepare for everything?

_____

7. Did you knew that yesterday was my birthday?

_____

8. She had already spoke with him yesterday.

_____

9. He do push-ups every day.

_____

10. I have been taken lessons here for three years.

_____

11. I had ate most of the food before she arrived.

_____

12. If they do not passed the exam they will have to retake it.

_____

Exercise 3: Irregular Verbs

Directions: Circle the past participle(s) or past tense verbs in each sentence, and make any necessary corrections.

1. Elisha could never have went to the state finals if I had not convinced her to join the team in the first place.

2. In retrospect, it seems I might have took too much time on the essay portion of the test.

3. While we played video games, Danny lay on the couch all afternoon.

4. Most people find it amazing that, millions of years ago, life sprung from a primordial swamp.

5. After we had placed our bets, we lay our cards on the table.

6. Carl would have tore his uniform if he had not stopped his slide at the last second.

7. The generals forsook their own troops in order to surrender and save their own lives.

8. When the temperature sunk below zero, the pipes bursted like water balloons.

9. The assets of the company were froze as soon as it declared bankruptcy.

10. Promptly at 6 o'clock, the assistant cook rung the bell for dinner, and the whole camp raced up the hill.

11. I was concerned about buying a cotton warm-up suit, and sure enough, it shrunk two sizes after the first wash.

12. By the time they pitched camp for the night, they had ridden over 30 miles.

13. George needed his friends more than ever, but they had forsook him.

14. We sung just about every song we know, then we went to bed.

Unauthorized copying or reuse of any part of this page is illegal.

Version 1.3

15. The senator could have spoke a lot longer, but she yielded the floor to her colleague.

Exercise 4

Correct all wrong-tense errors. If you can find nothing wrong with the sentence, write NO ERROR.

1. Since the state's economic troubles make it ripe for political change, many incumbent lawmakers might have soon found themselves out of a job.

_____

_____

2. If the terrorists instill fear in the heart of every citizen, they brought the city's normal life to a halt.

_____

_____

3. The Senator, already embroiled in a political scandal, resigned when news of his latest affair has been leaked to the press.

_____

_____

4. As the newly elected president took office, rebels in a far flung corner of the country, seeking to install a Marxist regime and put themselves in power, are preparing his downfall.

_____

_____

5. By the time Alaric the Goth sacked Rome in the early 5th century A.D., the city has become a mere shadow of its former self.

_____

_____

6. He told me that he was ready to leave, but we did not actually leave the house until four o'clock, an hour later than the time we had agreed upon.

_____

_____

7. In the late 1950s, Martin Luther King Jr., having won a great victory for desegregation during the Montgomery Bus Boycott, would have prepared to spread the movement for integration throughout the South.

_____

_____

8. For nearly a century, from the Napoleonic wars to the First World War, Europe has had but one major conflict fought on its soil.

_____

_____

9. Nowadays, with the emergence of the 70-hour work week, people became increasingly alienated from their neighbors and families.

_____

_____

10. In his farewell address, Washington asserted that the United States had to avoid permanent alliances with other nations that will risk dragging the young country into unnecessary wars.

_____

_____

Yellow Grammar 5

Mixed Practice

<u>Improving Sentences</u>

Directions: The following sentences test correctness and effectiveness of expression. Part of each sentence or the entire sentence is underlined; beneath each sentence are five ways of phrasing the underlined material. Choice **A** repeats the original phrasing; the other four choices are different. If you think the original phrasing produces a better sentence than any of the alternatives, select choice **A**; if not, select one of the other choices.

1. In *War and Peace*, Tolstoy presented his theories on history, and <u>illustrated them</u> with a slanted account of actual historical events.

   A. illustrated them

   B. also illustrating them

   C. he also was illustrating these ideas

   D. then illustrated the theories also

   E. then he went about illustrating them

2. In the United States, an increasing number of commuters <u>that believe their families to be</u> immune from the perils of city life.

   A. that believe their families to be

   B. that believe their families are

   C. believes their families are

   D. who believe their families to be

   E. believe their families to be

3. <u>Developed by a scientific team at his university</u>, the president informed the reporters that the new process would facilitate the diagnosis of certain congenital diseases.

   A. Developed by a scientific team at his university

   B. Having been developed by a scientific team at his university

   C. Speaking of the discovery made by a scientific team at his university

   D. Describing the development of a scientific team at his university

   E. As it had been developed by a scientific team at his university

4. The Equal Rights Amendment to Islandia's constitution is dying a lingering political death, <u>many dedicated groups and individuals have attempted</u> to prevent its demise.

   A. many dedicated groups and individuals have attempted

   B. although many dedicated groups and individuals have attempted

   C. many dedicated groups and persons has attempted

   D. despite many dedications of groups and individuals to attempt

   E. also, many dedicated groups and individuals have attempted

5. Developing a suitable environment for house plants <u>is in many ways like when you are managing</u> soil fertilization for city parks.

   A. is in many ways like when you are managing

   B. is in many ways similar to when you are managing

   C. in many ways is on a par with managing your

   D. is in many ways similar to the managing of

   E. is in many ways like managing

6. Most students would get better grades if <u>writing were to be studied by them</u>.

   A. writing were to be studied by them

   B. they studied writing

   C. writing was studied by them

   D. they would have studied writing

   E. they were to have studied writing

7. <u>If they do not go into bankruptcy</u>, the company will probably survive its recent setbacks.

   A. If they do not go into bankruptcy

   B. Unless bankruptcy cannot be avoided

   C. If they can avoid bankruptcy

   D. If bankruptcy will be avoided

   E. Unless it goes bankrupt

8. Now that I have read the works of both Henry and William James, I am convinced that Henry is <u>the best psychologist and William the best writer</u>.

   A. the best psychologist and William is the best writer

   B. a better psychologist, William is the best writer

   C. the best as a psychologist, William the test as a writer

   D. the best psychologist, William the better writer

   E. the better psychologist and William the better writer

9. When he arrived at the hospital, the doctor found that <u>several emergency cases had been admitted before</u> he went on duty.

A. several emergency cases had been admitted before

B. there were several emergency cases admitted prior to

C. two emergency cases were being admitted before

D. a couple of emergency cases were admitted before

E. several emergency cases was admitted before

10. The variety of Scandinavian health care services offered to residents at reduced cost <u>far exceeds low-cost health programs</u> available in the United States.

A. far exceeds low-cost health programs

B. far exceeds the number of low-cost health programs

C. tends to be greater than low-cost programs

D. far exceed the number of low-cost health programs

E. are greater than comparable low-cost health programs

Directions: The following sentences test your ability to recognize grammar and usage errors. Each sentence contains either a single error or no error at all. No sentence contains more than one error. The error, if there is one, will be underlined and lettered. If the sentence contains an error, select the letter of the incorrect portion. If the sentence is correct, select choice **E**.

1. Before <u>the advent of</u> modern surgical techniques, <u>bleeding patients</u> with leeches <u>were considered</u>
        A   B   C

   therapeutically <u>effective</u>.   <u>No Error</u>
                D   E

2. The <u>recent</u> establishment of "Crime Busters," officially sanctioned neighborhood block-watching
        A

   groups, <u>has</u> <u>dramatic</u> improved relations <u>between</u> citizens and police. <u>No error</u>
        B   C   D   E

3. <u>Lost in the forest</u> on a cold night, <u>the hunters built</u> a fire <u>to keep themselves</u> warm and <u>to frighten</u>
        A   B   C   D

   <u>away</u> the wolves. <u>No Error</u>
                  E

4. The effort to <u>create appropriate</u> theatrical effects <u>often result</u> in settings that cannot be <u>effective</u>
                A   B   C

   without an imaginative <u>lighting</u> crew. <u>No Error</u>
                     D   E

5. Every one of the shops in the town <u>were closed</u> on Thursday <u>because</u> of the <u>ten-inch</u> rainfall that
                                  A   B   C

   <u>had fallen</u> during the day. <u>No Error</u>
      D   E

6. <u>According to</u> the directions on the package, the contents <u>are</u> intended for external use <u>only</u>, and
        A   B   C

   <u>should not hardly</u> be swallowed, even in small quantities. <u>No Error</u>
      D   E

7. Mr. Webster's paper is <u>highly imaginary</u> and <u>very creative</u>, <u>but</u> seems to be <u>lacking in</u> cogency.
                             A   B   C   D

   <u>No Error</u>
     E

8. The late president's <u>numerous</u> memoirs now <u>about to be</u> published <u>promises</u> to be of special <u>his-</u>
                   A   B   C

   <u>torical</u> interest. <u>No Error</u>
      D   E

9. The point <u>on issue</u> was whether the dock workers, <u>who</u> were <u>an extremely</u> vocal group, <u>would de-</u>
               A   B   C   D
    <u>cide to</u> return to work.   <u>No Error</u>
                              E

10. <u>Raising</u> living costs, <u>together</u> with escalating taxes, <u>have</u> proved to be a burden for <u>everyone</u>.
     A   B   C   D
    <u>No Error</u>
       E

Improving Paragraphs

Directions: Read each passage and select the best answers for the questions that follow. Some questions are about particular sentences or parts of sentences and ask you to improve sentence structure or word choice, while other questions ask you to consider organization and development.

Questions 21-25 are based on the following essay, which is a response to an assignment to write about an economic issue facing the United States.

> **(1)** Last year, my social studies class attended a talk given by a young woman who worked in a factory in Central America making shirts for a popular U.S. retail chain. **(2)** The working conditions she described were horrific. **(3)** She spoke of being forced to work 14-hour days and even longer on weekends. **(4)** The supervisors often hit her and the other women, most of whom were teenagers, to get them to work faster. **(5)** They gave them contaminated water to drink and were only allowed to go to the bathroom twice a day. **(6)** She urged us to boycott the retail chain and to inform consumers about the conditions in their factories.
>
> **(7)** A group of us decided to meet with a representative of the chain and we would discuss our concerns and would announce our plans to boycott. **(8)** The representative said that low wages were necessary to keep costs down. **(9)** And she claimed a boycott would never work because it would be impossible to stop people from shopping at such a popular store. **(10)** "Nobody is going to listen to a bunch of teenagers," she said. **(11)** We decided to prove her wrong.
>
> **(12)** First, we calculated that the workers' wages accounted for less than one percent of the price people paid the shirts in the United States. **(13)** We argued that if the chain were willing to make slightly lower profits, it could afford to pay the workers more without raising prices. **(14)** And when we began informing people about the conditions under which the shirts they bought were made, they were horrified. **(15)** Many were agreeing to shop there no longer, they even wrote letters to the president of the chain in which he was urged to do something about the conditions in the factories. **(16)** Even local politicians got involved. **(17)** The winner of that year's City Council election pledged to change the conditions in the factories or shut the store down once and for all. **(18)** Finally, with business almost at a standstill, the store agreed to consumers' demands.

1. In context, which is the best version of the underlined portion of sentence 5 (reproduced below)?

   They gave them contaminated water to drink <u>and were only allowed to go</u> to the bathroom twice a day.

   A. (As it is now)

   B. and were only allowing them to go

   C. and only allowed them to go

   D. and they were only given permission to go

   E. and were allowed to only go

2. In context, which of the following best replaces the word "their" in sentence 6 (reproduced below)?

   She urged us to boycott the retail chain and to inform consumers about the conditions in their factories.

   A. the consumers'

   B. it's

   C. the workers'

   D. the company's

   E. the students'

3. Which of the following versions of the underlined portion of sentence 7 (reproduced below) is best?

   A group of us decided to meet with a representative of the chain <u>and we would discuss our concerns and would announce</u> our plans to boycott.

   A. (As it is now)

   B. to discuss our concerns and announce

   C. for the purpose of discussing our concerns and announcing

   D. where we would discuss our concerns and announce

   E. with whom we would be discussing our concerns and to whom we would announce

4. Which of the following would be the best replacement for the word "And" at the beginning of sentence 9 (reproduced below)?

   And she claimed a boycott would never work because it would be impossible to stop people from shopping at such a popular store.

   A. Moreover,

   B. Rather,

   C. However,

   D. Even so,

   E. Instead,

5. In context, which of the following is the best way to revise the underlined portion of sentence 15 (reproduced below)?

Many were agreeing to shop there no longer, they even wrote letters to the president of the chain in which he was urged to do something about the conditions in the factories.

    A. (As it is now)

    B. Many agreed to no longer shop there and even writing letters to the president of the chain to urge him

    C. Agreeing to shop there no longer, many even wrote letters to the president of the chain urging him

    D. Many agreed to no longer shop there and also to urge the president of the chain by writing letters in which they asked him

    E. Shopping there no longer, many agreed to write letters to the president of the chain to urge him

Homework

<u>Sentence Error</u>

Read and answer the questions below. On the right-hand side of the paper, write what is wrong with the sentence in your own words.

1. <u>Being that</u> my car is getting <u>its</u> annual tune-up,
     A   B
I <u>will not be</u> able to <u>pick you up</u> tomorrow morn
   C   D
ing. <u>No Error</u>
     E

2. The teacher <u>with her capable aides</u> <u>have com</u>
                   A   B
<u>plete control</u> of the situation; I <u>look forward</u> to a
                             C
very <u>uneventful</u> trip. <u>No Error</u>
     D   E

3. We <u>can't hardly</u> believe that the situation is <u>so</u>
      A   B
<u>serious as</u> to justify such precautions as you <u>have</u>
     C   D
<u>taken</u>. <u>No Error</u>
       E

4. No one <u>but</u> <u>he</u> knew <u>which</u> questions <u>were go</u>
        A B   C   D
ing to be asked on this test. <u>No Error</u>
                       E

5. You are being <u>quite</u> cynical when you say <u>that</u>
               A   B
<u>the reason</u> we have <u>such a large</u> turnout <u>is be</u>
                    C   D
cause we are serving refreshments. <u>No Error</u>
                              E

 **C2 education** be smarter.

Unauthorized copying or reuse of any part of this page is illegal.

Version 1.3

Improving Sentences

Read and answer the questions below. On the right-hand side of the paper, write what is wrong with the original sentence in your own words.

1. Although serfs were lucky to drink their ale form cracked wooden bowls, nobles customarily <u>drunk their wine from</u> elaborately chased drinking horns.

   (A) drunk their wine from

   (B) have drinked their wine from

   (C) drank their wine from

   (D) had drunken their wine from

   (E) drinking their wine from

2. Before the search party reached the scene of the accident, <u>the rain began to fall</u>, making rescue efforts more difficult.

   (A) the rain began to fall

   (B) the rain had began to fall

   (C) it began to rain

   (D) the rain had begun to fall

   (E) it started to rain

3. For many students, <u>keeping a journal during college seems satisfying their need</u> for self-expression.

   (A) keeping a journal during college seems satisfying their need

   (B) keeping a journal during college seems to satisfy their need

   (C) keeping a journal during college seeming satisfying their need

   (D) to keep a journal during college seems satisfying their need

   (E) the keeping of a journal during college seems to satisfy their need

4. Peter Martin began to develop his own choreographic <u>style, but he was able</u> to free himself from the influence of Balanchine.

   (A) style, but he was able to

   (B) style; but he was able to

   (C) style only when he was able to

   (D) style only when he is able to

   (E) style: only when he was able to

   (F)

5. <u>Irregardless of the outcome</u> of this dispute, our two nations will remain staunch allies.

   (A) Irregardless of the outcome

   (B) Regardless of how the outcome

   (C) With regard to the outcome

   (D) Regardless of the outcome

   (E) Disregarding the outcome

Improving Paragraphs

Read the short essay below. Use the lines provided to write 5 things that could be done to improve the essay. These things may include combining sentences, moving sentences, deleting sentences, or revising them.

(1) In the 1930s, the film industry was just beginning its journey. (2) It would become an American institution. (3) In its early years, though, there were setbacks and speedbumps. (4) One of the most famous was the Motion Picture Production Code. (5) This was also known as the Hays Code. (6) The man who came up with the code was named Hays.

(7) This code, created to police morality in movies, were instated in 1930. (8) The code banned all mentions of what it called "immoral activities." (9) By 1968, the code was abolished. (10) This included any references to homosexuality, or other such controversial topics. (11) The code insisted that criminals always be punished for their crimes, and so the villains must never be sympathetic to the audience. (12) As well, authority figures must always be respected and members of the clergy must never be portrayed as a villain or a comic character. (13) The code even banned mention of mixed-race couples, which to some was an offensive idea.

(14) For one, many filmmakers said that the Code preempted their right to free speech. (15) There were many criticisms of the Hays Code. (16) One famous publication, *The Nation*, said of the code, "if crime is never presented in a sympathetic light, then taken literally that would mean that "law and justice" would become one and the same. (17) Therefore, events such as the Boston Tea Party could not be portrayed." (18) Nowadays there are much fewer rules. (19) The right of filmmakers to have his or her voices heard has been defended.

1. _____
   _____
   _____
   _____

2. _____
   _____
   _____
   _____

3. _____
   _____
   _____
   _____

4. _____
   _____
   _____
   _____

5. _____
   _____
   _____
   _____

Yellow Grammar 6

Subject/Verb Agreement I

Introduction

When solving a subject/verb agreement problem on the SAT, the first thing you need to do is to identify the subject and the verb in the sentence. Then you need to decide whether the subject is singular or plural.

Singular Subjects

A singular subject needs a singular verb.

Kevin *listens* carefully. ("Kevin" is the singular subject, and "listens" is the singular verb.)

Remember, many singular verbs end in "s." Most singular nouns do not end in "s."

Gina *walks* quickly.

Tim *goes* mountain climbing every weekend.

The **student** *is* tall.

This **dog** *does* not like ice cream.

However, there are exceptions. A singular noun that ends in "s" (such as a class name or a book title) also needs a singular verb that ends in "s."

Physics *deals* with practical topics.

Uglies *is* one of my favorite books.

Collective nouns are singular nouns that represent a group of people, things, etc. Even though collective nouns represent multiple people or things, they are singular nouns and need singular verbs.

The book **club** *meets* at the library.

The **orchestra** *rehearses* in the auditorium.

The **family** *eats* at the diner.

The **staff** *celebrates* holidays together.

The **class** *meets* at the community center on Tuesdays.

Plural Subjects

A plural subject needs a plural verb.

The **dancers** *are* graceful. ("Dancers" is the plural subject, and "are" is the plural verb.)

Remember, many plural nouns end in "s." Most plural verbs do <u>not.</u>

Students *sing* in the choir.

Students *do* not like exams.

Artists *work* in this studio.

Teachers *go* to that training seminar.

However, there are exceptions. Not all plural nouns in end in "s."

They *listen* carefully.

People *walk* to the festival.

Children *watch* movies.

Compound Subjects

Some sentences have **compound subjects** – two or more subjects to which one verb applies. Determining the form of the verb depends upon how the subjects are joined. Subjects joined by "and" need a plural verb.

David <u>and</u> **Juan** *need* to go to the store.

Students <u>and</u> **teachers** *like* summer vacation.

Some subjects are joined by "or" or "nor." In these sentences, the verb must agree with the subject that is *closest* to it in the sentence.

Neither **David** nor **Juan** *needs* to buy milk. ("Needs" must agree with "Juan," a singular subject.)

Neither the **teacher** nor the **students** *need* to remember the tickets. ("Needs" must agree with "students," a plural subject.)

Either **Lila** or **Dan** *bakes* the cakes. ("Bakes" must agree with Dan, a singular subject.)

Other Situations

There are times when the subject and the verb are not right next to each other in the sentence. Sometimes they are separated by phrases.

Animals in the jungle **are** camouflaged.

The **girls** on my team **think** we will win the competition.

My **friend** down the street **enjoys** running.

These sentences have *prepositional phrases* between the subject and the verb. Take a look at the first sentence. Though the object of the preposition ("jungle") may be singular, you need to remember that the SUBJECT ("animals") remains plural, and thus the verb ("are") should be plural as well.

Now look at these sentences:

Burt Billingsley, together with the Action 5 News Team, is dedicated to bringing you today's news.

The American auto industry, as well as the construction industry, has suffered some setbacks.

Phrases such as "together with," "along with," "as well as," and "in addition to" may come between a subject and its verb, but they DO NOT change the relationship between the subject and its verb. A singular subject will need a singular verb and a plural subject will need a plural verb. Don't allow distracting phrases to throw you off.

Finally, you may run across **inverted sentences** – in which the subject comes AFTER the verb. (Questions count as inverted sentences as well.)

On the bus **are** many **students**. (Reword this in your head. Many **students** *are* on the bus.)

Are the **students finished** with the test? (Reword this in your head. The **students** *are* finished with the test.)

Exercise 1

Directions: Correct the error in each sentence. If there is none, write "no error."

1. One of the main reasons he donated the books and magazines were that he had already read each one several times.

_____

_____

2. The cooking class, taught by several of the Culinary Institute's master chefs, were prepared to dazzle the critics.

_____

_____

3. Documents containing lists of names of people who collaborated with the former communist regime has recently been de-classified by the government.

_____

_____

Unauthorized copying or reuse of any part of this page is illegal.

Version 1.3

4. Despite my wishes, neither my brother nor my sister were willing to do my chores for me during my absence.

_____

_____

5. The number of mistakes committed by players during yesterday's workouts are outrageous.

_____

_____

6. The compromise settled upon by the august senators were the reason that a temporary peace was achieved.

_____

_____

7. The delivery of the construction materials, scheduled for this Thursday, have been delayed due to unexpected transportation and maintenance fees.

_____

_____

8. Neither the illustrious Dr. Roberts nor his protégé Samuel Stevens were able to discern the root cause of the disease.

_____

_____

9. The only thing that can prevent Sam and Tommy from deserting the dinner table after finishing their vegetables are either chocolate mousse or ice cream cake.

_____

_____

10. Next to his stamp collection sits the boy's favorite stuffed animals—Harry the Duck and Weasel the Walrus-Man.

_____

_____

11. The beauty of the churches and monasteries in the Balkans are attributable in large measure to Byzantine cultural and economic influences.

_____

_____

12. Taking full account of our financial problems, which have been looming over our heads these last few months, are quite depressing.

_____

_____

13. The society that evolved in Europe after the fall of the Old Roman Empire and during the early centuries of the Middle Ages were at once reflective of and divorced from Roman ideals.

_____

_____

14. The chemical waste that has been dumped into the river over the last fifty years by petrochemical and oil companies have had devastating consequences for the region's wildlife.

_____

_____

15. Describing one's emotions are sometimes an extremely difficult task that leaves one feeling empty and frustrated.

_____

_____

Unauthorized copying or reuse of any part of this page is illegal.

Version 1.3

16. Along this old road stands several well-preserved medieval stone dwellings, which, because of their circular design, are unique in Europe.

_____

_____

17. A debate concerning the desirability of reinstituting the draft and expanding our military capabilities more generally has sprung up all across the country.

_____

_____

18. Patience, as well as an unswerving attention to the fundamentals of baseball, have always characterized Tony Gwyn's approach to hitting.

_____

_____

19. The adversarial relationship between lions and other cats of the savannah are directly linked to the matter of territorial rights.

_____

_____

20. Requiring employees to enter both a password and a security code each time they log into the computer network have helped protect clients' accounts.

_____

_____

Exercise 2

Directions: Underline the italicized verbs in the sentences that contain errors in subject-verb agreement.

1. According to a noted meteorologist, there *is* various explanations for the accelerating rate of global warming.

2. In this critically acclaimed film, there *is* a well-developed plot and an excellent cast of characters.

3. Through the locks of the Panama Canal *passes* more than fifty ships each day.

4. There *are* a number of state legislatures currently debating strict environmental laws.

5. If there *is* competing proposals, your idea may not be acted upon until next week.

6. There *is* at least five types of climbing rose and a unique variety of small fir in the Botanical Gardens.

7. Despite numerous professed sightings, there *is* still no conclusive evidence of extraterrestrial beings.

Exercise 3

Directions: Underline the verb that agrees with the subject.

1. Multipurpose vehicles, which can be very useful on rough terrain, (is/are) now banned in many states.

2. The level of chemicals and other air pollutants (is/are) now monitored in many offices.

3. The fundamental hitting skills of Rick Reuschel (goes/go) largely unnoticed by the average fan.

Version 1.3

4. A community as diverse as Los Angeles (attracts/attract) immigrants from many countries.

5. One-way tickets for domestic travel (is/are) often more expensive than round-trip fares.

6. So-called "bullet trains" from Tokyo to Osaka (completes/complete) the 300-mile trip in about two hours.

7. Donations to the church-sponsored orphanage (is/are) up by 50 percent over last year.

8. Einstein's theory of relativity (ranks/rank) with the most developed hypotheses involving space and time.

Exercise 4

Directions: Underline the verb that agrees with the true subject.

1. The fishing industry, along with railroad safety issues, (is/are) of great concern to the state assembly.

2. Either the manager or one of his coaches usually (removes/remove) a pitcher from the mound.

3. Both the word scuba and the word radar (is/are) acronyms.

4. Auto exhaust, in addition to industrial pollution, (is/are) a cause of smog in southern California.

5. It is said that neither poor weather nor poor health (keeps/keep) a postman from making his rounds.

Homework: Subject/Verb Agreement

Directions: Correct the error in each sentence. If there is none, write "no error."

1. In Kurt Vonnegut's novel *Slaughterhouse-Five*, the tales of the bombing of Dresden during World War II is rather chilling.

_____

_____

2. There has been, according to the Council for the Preservation of Marine Life, only seventeen known sting ray attacks worldwide since 1996.

_____

_____

3. Around the earth orbits more than fifty state-of-the-art satellites, a few of which are used for spying.

_____

_____

4. Since the issue was hotly debated, there were neither a consensus nor even a calm discussion at the town meeting tonight.

_____

_____

5. Neither of the delegates sent by the president to negotiate the peace treaty have a background in diplomacy.

_____

_____

Unauthorized copying or reuse of any part of this page is illegal.

Version 1.3

6. The aircraft carriers Lincoln and Washington, supposedly the main targets of the attack, was, luckily, out to sea when the air raid began.

_____

_____

7. Every Saturday morning the pleasing aroma of sizzling bacon and waffles spread throughout Jane and Randolph's apartment.

_____

_____

8. Sir Anthony Hopkins, despite starring mainly in Hollywood films over the last twenty years, embody the greatness of Britain's long and storied theater tradition.

_____

_____

9. Her desire to become a doctor, the driving force behind Jane's strong work ethic and enthusiasm for school, keeps her focused and out of trouble.

_____

_____

10. Creating strife among the staff members, a favorite pastime of Samuel and James, infuriate everyone in the office.

_____

_____

11. In the city of Pola sit many Roman-era structures, including a remarkably well-preserved arena from the second-century A.D.

_____

_____

12. The wealth of the citizens of these towns are a source of pride for some, a cause of resentment for others.

_____

_____

13. The excuse for their tardiness given by the normally punctual students have satisfied the teacher, who is lenient with students as long as they are honest.

_____

_____

14. The desire to "keep up with the Jones's"—that is, to keep pace with one's neighbors— have been cited as a major source of stress for many Americans.

_____

_____

15. The current debate over whether it should be permissible to use embryonic stem cells for research purposes are likely to remain a hot topic for years to come.

_____

_____

16. Roger's talent for assembling machines and other contraptions have led teachers to encourage him to pursue a career in engineering.

_____

_____

17. Each of the players involved in the melee last Saturday evening have been fined an undisclosed amount of money.

_____

_____

18. Jill's hard work, in addition to her cleverness and ability to learn from mistakes, lift her to the top of the class.

_____

_____

19. These professors, as wise and learned as any the world has to offer, raises the level of academic rigor in the philosophy department to amazing heights.

_____

_____

20. At the summit of the mountain stands a monument to the former Soviet leader and the decaying remains of a medieval castle.

_____

_____

Yellow Grammar 7

Pronouns I

Introduction

A **pronoun** is a word that is used in place of a noun. The **antecedent** of a pronoun is the word to which the pronoun refers.

Example: <u>Mary</u> was late for work because <u>she</u> forgot to set the alarm.

        ANTECEDENT   PRONOUN

Occasionally, an antecedent will appear in a sentence after the pronoun.

Example: Because <u>he</u> sneezes so often, <u>Arthur</u> always thinks <u>he</u> might have the flu.

       PRONOUN   ANTECEDENT   PRONOUN

Pronouns and Agreement

A definite pronoun must clearly refer to, and agree with, its antecedent.

Number Agreement

Pronouns must agree in number with their antecedents. A singular pronoun should stand in for a singular antecedent. A plural pronoun should stand in for a plural antecedent. Here's a typical SAT pronoun error.

WRONG: The bank turned Harry down when he applied for a loan because <u>their</u> credit department discovered that he didn't have a job.

What does the plural possessive *their* refer to? The singular collective noun *bank*. The singular possessive *its* is what we need here.

RIGHT: The bank turned Harry down for a loan because **its** credit department discovered that he didn't have a job.

Exercise 1: Pronoun in the Wrong Number

Directions: Are the following sentences grammatically correct? Mark the incorrect sentences and replace the italicized words with the correct forms using the blank lines.

1. The appreciation shown to the dance troupe was a symbol of the school's gratitude for *their* _____ hard work.

2. The mayor welcomed the foreign delegation by presenting *them* _____ with a key to the city.

3. Crowds of tennis fans love his style of play, because the tennis star frequently appeals to *them* _____ for support.

4. The Internal Revenue Service is annually derided by critics who claim that *their* _____ instruction manuals for filing taxes are too cryptic.

5. A typical bank will reject an application for a loan if *their* _____ credit department discovers that the applicant is unemployed.

6. Investors who lost money in the stock market crash generally recouped *his* _____ losses over the next 18 months.

7. The committee asserts that the venture capitalist has not proven quite as philanthropic as *their* _____ public relations campaign suggests.

8. The waitresses in this elegant restaurant can receive up to eighty percent of *her* _____ salary in tips.

Person Agreement/Pronoun Shift

Pronouns must agree with their antecedents in person. A first-person pronoun should stand in for a first-person antecedent, and so on.

WRONG: Paul, Billy and I walked to the seats reserved for <u>them</u>.

"Paul, Billy and I," the subject, should be changed into a plural first-person pronoun, since the speaker ("I") is included in the subject. Thus, the pronoun shouldn't be *them*, it should be *us*.

RIGHT: Paul, Billy and I walked to the seats reserved for <u>us</u>.

When a sentence changes pronoun number or person midway through, that is called *pronoun shift*. It is always considered an error.

WRONG: When you prepare this meal, <u>one</u> must be careful not to burn the crust.

RIGHT: When you prepare this meal, <u>you</u> must be careful not to burn the crust.

One more thing to remember about which pronoun to use with which antecedent: Never use the relative pronoun *which* to refer to a human being. Use *who, whom* or *that*.

WRONG: The woman **which** is standing at the piano is my sister.

RIGHT: The woman **who** is standing at the piano is my sister.

Exercise 2: Pronoun Shift

Directions: Identify the sentences that include a pronoun shift and replace the incorrect italicized words with the correct forms, using the blanks.

1. When we gather during the Thanksgiving holidays, *you* _____ cannot help appreciating family and friends.

2. One cannot gauge the immensity of the Empire State Building until *you* _____ *stand* atop the building.

3. As you arrive in New York City's Grand Central Terminal, *one* _____ can easily imagine that station as the most elaborate in all of the United States.

4. You may not be fond of Shakespeare, but the theater company guarantees *you* _____*will* be impressed with the quality of acting in this production.

5. You should not even attempt to pass your driving test unless *one* _____ *has* learned to parallel park.

6. When they grew up in my grandfather's neighborhood during the Great Depression, *you* _____ could feel the despair that gripped the nation.

7. Whenever we read about a plane crash, even as an infrequent flyer, *one* _____ *becomes* concerned about air safety.

8. When one considers the vastness of the universe, one cannot help being struck by *your* _____ own insignificance.

Pronouns and Case

A more subtle type of pronoun problem is one in which the pronoun is in the wrong case. Look at the following chart:

	Number and Person			Case	
	Singular	**Plural**		**Subjective**	**Objective**
First Person	I, me	we, us			
	my, mine	our, ours	**First Person**	I	me
				we	us
Second Person	you	you			
	your, yours	your, your	**Second Person** you you	you	you
Third Person	he, him	they, them			
	she, her		**Third Person**	he	him
	it			she	her
	one			it	they
	his	their, theirs		they	them
	her, hers			one	one
	its				
	one's		**Relative**	who	whom
			Pronouns	that	that
				which	which

When to Use Subjective Case Pronouns

Use a subjective case pronoun as the subject of a sentence.

> Example: **She** is falling asleep.

> WRONG: Nancy, Claire, and **me** are going to the ballet.

> RIGHT: Nancy, Claire, and **I** are going to the ballet.

Use the subjective case after a linking verb like *to be*.

> Example: It is **I**.

Use the subjective case in comparisons between the subject of verbs that are not stated, but understood.

> Example: Gary is taller than **they** (are).

When to Use Objective Case Pronouns

Use an objective case pronoun as the object of a verb.

> Example: I called **her**.

Use the objective case for the object of a preposition.

> Example: I laughed at **him**.

Use the objective case after infinitives and gerunds.

> Example: Asking **him** to go was a big mistake.

> Example: To give **him** the scare of his life, we all jumped out of his closet.

Use the objective case in comparisons between objects of verbs that are not stated but understood.

> Example: She calls you more than (she calls) **me**.

Exercise 2: Pronoun in the Wrong Case

Directions: Underline the pronoun that makes the sentence grammatically correct.

1. The other drivers and (I/me) pulled over until the heavy rains passed.
2. I did not receive the final draft of the report until it was approved by my supervisor and (he/him).
3. (We/Us) and the high school band accompanied the team to the stadium on the chartered bus.
4. Our professor forgot to distribute the new Bunsen burner kit to my lab partner and (I/me).
5. (She/Her) and her parents set off yesterday on a three-week cruise of the North Atlantic.
6. It was surprising to hear the minister address my new wife and (I/me) as "Mr. and Mrs. Murphy."
7. The legal authorities questioned (she/her) and the other students involved in the incident for two hours before dropping the charges.
8. (We/Us) and the other team combined for 16 runs and 23 hits in the seven-inning game.

Who and Whom

An important distinction to make is between the relative pronoun *who* (subjective case: *he, she, etc.*) and the relative pronoun *whom* (objective case: *whom* goes with *him* and *them*). For example, would you know which of those pronouns to use in the following sentence?

Sylvester, (who or whom?) is afraid of the dark, sleeps with a Donald Duck night-light on.

The following method can help you decide when to use *whom* and when to use *who*.

First, start by looking only at the relative pronoun in its clause. Ignore the rest of the sentence.

Sylvester, **(who or whom?) is afraid of the dark**, sleeps with a Donald Duck night-light on.

Then, turn the clause into a question:

Who or whom is afraid of the dark?

Answer the question with an ordinary personal pronoun.

He is.

If you've answered the question with a subjective case pronoun (as you have here), you need the subjective case who in the relative clause.

Sylvester, **who** is afraid of the dark, sleeps with a Donald Duck night-light on.

If you answer the question with an objective case pronoun, you need the objective case *whom* in the relative clause.

HINT: Try answering the question with *he* or *him*. *Who* goes with *he* (subjective case) and *whom* goes with *him* (objective case).

Pronoun Reference

Finally, a pronoun should clearly refer to its antecedent. If the sentence is poorly worded, some ambiguity is created:

The producer told the director that **he** had made a huge mistake during the filming.

Who is "he" in this sentence? Is it the producer? The director? The way this sentence is written, the reader can't be sure. If there is a definite pronoun in the sentence that cannot be tracked back to an antecedent, you have an error. One common pronoun reference error is the overuse of "they", as seen below:

Tom likes to go to the open-air market where **they** call out prices and display food in the stalls.

Who are "they"? Yes, logically, you can assume that "they" are the sellers in the open-air market.

However, the sentence doesn't tell us this explicitly... thus, according to the SAT, it's an error. If you see an unnamed "they," you have an error on your hands.

> CORRECT: Tom likes to go to the open-air market where the sellers call out prices and display food in the stalls.

Exercise 4: Unclear Pronoun Reference

Directions: Read the following sentences and circle the pronouns with ambiguous reference.

1. The company chairman contacted the marketing director after he failed to attend the sales meeting.

2. Temporary loss of hearing is a common occurrence at rock concerts where they sit too close to the mammoth speakers.

3. The small claims court lawyer won the case for the defendant once she proved her innocence with legal documents.

4. Jurors are told to disregard the race of the participants in a trial when they come into the courtroom.

5. When an old friend came to town last week, he asked what plays they were presenting on Broadway.

6. The manager benched the star player after he criticized the pitcher's lack of intensity.

7. Dozens of students rallied against administration officials to protest the music they were playing on the college radio station.

8. When the painters work on your neighbors' laundry room, make sure that they do not get paint on their clothes.

Indefinite Pronouns

We've talked about objective pronouns and subjective pronouns. However, all those are DEFINITE pronouns – they have an antecedent. Another type of pronoun, the **indefinite pronoun**, does not. Below is a list of indefinite pronouns:

> Singular: another, anybody, anyone, anything, each, either, everybody, everyone, everything, little, much, neither, nobody, no one, nothing, one, other, somebody, someone, something

> Plural: both, few, many, others, several

> Singular or Plural: all, any, more, most, none, some

The important thing to remember with indefinite pronouns is their number. That can be a little tricky

because even though most indefinite pronouns are either singular or plural, a few are both. For example, as noted earlier the indefinite pronoun *all* can be either plural or singular. Consider the following sentences:

All *of the cake* **was** eaten. All *of the soldiers* **were** ready to fight.

Did you notice that the first sentence used a singular verb, while the second sentence used a plural verb? Although both sentences start with the indefinite pronoun *all* the two sentences refer to different quantities. In the first sentence *all* of one cake *was* eaten, so the verb is singular. In the second sentence *all* refers to the plural *soldiers*, so the verb is plural. When you see or use indefinite pronouns that can be either singular or plural, always be aware of the quantity of the noun that follows that pronoun.

Recognizing indefinite pronouns that can only be singular or plural can also be challenging. Look at the following sentence. Why is it wrong? Each of the girls say that their coach is the best.

The sentence is wrong because "Each" is always singular. Thus, the verb "say" should be the singular form "says." Here's the corrected sentence:

Each of the girls says that her coach is the best.

Exercise 5: Indefinite Pronouns

Read the sentences below and determine if they are correctly written. Correct any errors you see.

1. Each of the players on the team practice every day.

2. Few people realize how hard we work.

3. Some of the roast turkey are missing.

4. All of the volunteers are invited to a celebration after the work is done.

5. Anyone attending the reading class need to do their homework before class starts.

6. Everything we saw were just amazing.

7. Others in the political party believes this is an unwise choice.

Exercise 6: Pronoun Case

Directions: Correct the error in each sentence. If there is none, write "no error."

1. No other employees have been informed yet that him and Thomas will soon be let go by the company.

_____

_____

2. The chief editor, displeased by the recent work of his regular editors, assigned the essays to Harriet and I.

_____

_____

3. Us tutors are prepared to assign homework, but only if the homework is relevant to the day's lesson.

_____

_____

4. The last political disagreement between him and I was whether the President should have the right to declare war without Congressional approval.

_____

_____

5. The scientists were amazed to learn that the chimpanzees handed the bananas to Lenny and I after the two of us had said that we were extremely hungry.

_____

_____

Version 1.3

6. Given the difficult financial situation in which we found ourselves, one could hardly blame either my spouse or I for being a bit irritable.

_____

_____

7. It is unlikely that you will find any weaklings among we muscular, weight-lifting men.

_____

_____

8. It is only fair that credit for coming up with this masterful design should be divided equally between my partner and I.

_____

_____

9. If you want to get your teeth truly clean, we dentists are the only ones who can make sure no plaque remains to decay your teeth's enamel.

_____

_____

10. With the exception of Paula and I, all trainers and assistant trainers are to arrive at the airport at no later than five o'clock.

_____

_____

Exercise 7: Pronoun Agreement

Directions: Correct the error in each sentence. If there is none, write "no error."

1. As one progresses through the various stages of the public speaking program, you will gain increasing confidence in speaking before large audiences.

_____

_____

2. The association of lawyers has claimed that they will reimburse those clients whose cases end in convictions.

_____

_____

3. When Eric the Viking arrived at a monastery, he would murder their inhabitants and plunder its riches for himself and his men.

_____

_____

4. Fearing that the police were going to destroy the museum, the head curators gathered the museum's precious artifacts and hid it in a secret location in a field next to the building.

_____

_____

5. Each of the various skull fragments was examined in terms of their resemblance to modern Caucasoid skull parts.

_____

_____

6. Juliet assembled all her old clothes and, with the help of her friend Susan, lugged it down to the Salvation Army building.

_____

_____

7. Each member of the fraternity was forced to sign a statement confessing their guilt and agreeing to compensate the university for any damages to university property.

_____

_____

8. The remains of the house, scattered throughout the neighborhood by the storm's heavy winds, were gathered in a massive pile before it was shipped off by clean-up crews.

_____

_____

9. The school board has publicly announced their intention to eliminate all school-funded extracurricular programs.

_____

_____

10. From the branches Rainsford fashioned several sharp stakes, which he then planted at the bottom of the pit where it could serve as a deathtrap for whoever should have the misfortune of falling in.

_____

_____

Homework: Pronouns

Exercise 1: Pronoun Case

Directions: Correct the error in each sentence. If there is none, write "no error."

1. The actors had worked hard all day, but still the director asked they to remain for an extra hour of rehearsal.

_____

_____

2. There are multiple reasons why the other students and me will not eat the cafeteria's so-called "mystery meat."

_____

_____

3. For our hard work and effort, the committee decided to award Student Athlete of the Month to both Doug and I.

_____

_____

4. Emily maintains that her and Simon are the most devoted Star Trek fans in the universe and that they have even decided to name their firstborn child Lt. Sulu.

_____

_____

5. Although it may appear otherwise, I never desired for either Brittney or he to learn of our secret undertakings.

_____

_____

6. The principal rebuked the delinquent boys for assaulting their teacher with a barrage of paper airplanes and then sentenced him to twenty-four hours of detention.

_____

_____

7. In order to avoid letting your mind wander when studying, one must keep a sharp focus and minimize external distractions.

_____

_____

8. Students are to collect all of the crayons and markers on the floor, then put it in the boxes on the shelves.

_____

_____

9. The U.S. national soccer team played with an energy that they lacked in the most recent World Cup tournament.

_____

_____

10. In its recent committee report, the senators advocated a change of course for American foreign policy, arguing that America's current direction was causing it to become increasingly isolated on the world stage.

_____

_____

Exercise 2: Pronoun Reference

1. Having always been intrigued by the work and lifestyle of archaeologists, Harrison would very much like to become one.

_____

_____

2. According to Jeff, his father appeared amazingly calm considering that he had just crashed the family car.

_____

_____

3. In twelve volumes of detailed research, they describe both the origins of the Roman Empire and the effects of its ultimate collapse.

_____

_____

4. The police decided to grant immunity to George and Everett if he would testify against the mastermind of the robbery.

_____

_____

5. Greatly envious of a professional golfer's lifestyle, Tommy spent hours on the practice range trying to perfect his swing and become one.

_____

_____

6. Mark is going to meet with Steve today to discuss those harsh comments he made at the family reunion last month.

_____

_____

Version 1.3

7. According to my sister, Emily and Jen are supposed to meet at their office to review the report Emily has just written.

_____

_____

8. In this article, it examines the current debate over that country's nuclear ambitions and the steps that should be taken by the international community to halt those efforts.

_____

_____

9. In my opinion, Samantha and Jane will never reconcile their differences until she admits that she was wrong and apologizes.

_____

_____

10. Professor Williams has done more research than either Professor James or Dr. Stevenson, but the students firmly maintain that he is the best lecturer of the three.

_____

_____

Yellow Grammar 8

Mixed Review

In this lesson, we will review a few of the concepts that you have already studied.

<u>Subject-Verb Agreement</u>

Directions: Correct the error in each sentence. If there is none, write "no error."

1. The number of mentally ill people imprisoned in state and federal penitentiaries have grown to an alarming extent over the last thirty years.

   _____

   _____

2. The search for a cure for AIDS, as well as the ongoing battles against cancer and other serious illnesses have not, despite decreased government funding for scientific research, slowed down at all.

   _____

   _____

3. Joseph, who often struggles to interact with his coworkers, like to sit quietly in the corner while everyone else mingles and networks.

   _____

   _____

4. Although only a scrap of the ancient texts remain, Professor Gager maintains that this historical source is invaluable to scholars of Christianity.

   _____

   _____

Version 1.3

5. At the other end of the city, near the United Nations offices, stands several fine examples of Tudor-style architecture.

_____

_____

6. The council of astronomers' recent decision to relegate Pluto to the status of "dwarf- planet" have generated relatively little controversy.

_____

_____

7. Confident that his time would come, Davis openly acknowledged there is many legitimate reasons why he had yet to win a gold medal.

_____

_____

8. Perched atop the highest tree branches lurk the hawk, eager to pounce on its helpless, unsuspecting prey.

_____

_____

9. The new building, though dubbed a "masterpiece" by a panel of leading critics and prominent architects, fails to meet the business's 21st century needs.

_____

_____

10. Since the book contained many confusing twists and turns, James felt lost as the spiritual guru lectured about the readings and were subsequently bewildered when the class ended.

_____

_____

11. The Chief Justice, who often writes the dissenting opinion to the court's conservative rulings, have won the hearts and minds of the liberal elite.

_____

_____

12. No report on casualties can be given at this point, as neither the captain nor the lieutenant have any idea how the battle ended

_____ ,

_____

13. The television series "Lost" focuses heavily on the complicated personal dramas that defines each of the characters' pasts.

_____

_____

14. Have there ever in the history of the world been anyone who could simultaneously tie his shoe and jump rope without falling over?

_____

_____

15. The president of the council, together with his counterparts in the other allied countries, has called for a withdrawal of the coalition's army.

_____

_____

16. Regular consumption of a variety of fruits and vegetables, in addition to frequent exercise and a stress-free lifestyle, are vital to one's long-term health.

_____

_____

17. For a variety of reasons, one of which is heightened public awareness of the appropriate safety measures, the number of shark attacks have fallen steadily over the last fifteen years.

_____

_____

18. The last thing the professors wanted to do in situations like those were to appear ignorant or out of touch with the student body.

_____

_____

19. Enclosed in the file is a training manual and a document that contains a description of the company's policy and goals.

_____

_____

20. The essay on humans' inherent tendency toward greed and selfishness only confirm my general belief that there are few benevolent forces acting in the world.

_____

_____

Practice: Identifying Parts of the Sentence

Read the sentences below. Circle the subject, underline the predicate, and draw a box around the object (if there is one).

1. Frank found the lighter in between the cushions of the couch.

2. Losing his breath, Aaron begged the others to wait up for him.

3. Production on the new line of cars has stopped because of product recalls.

4. Anyone who visits New York for the first time will be overwhelmed by the sights and sounds.

5. The most recent study has verified many scientists' theories.

6. Portia and Abby love the bakery's cinnamon loaves.

7. Many critics have called the director's latest movie "a masterpiece."

8. Anthony Portrato, the famous rock star, played a few songs before he signed autographs.

9. Practicing your piano work will improve your manual dexterity.

10. Congress has recently passed many landmark laws.

Now read the sentences below. Circle any adjectives, draw a box around any adverbs, and underline any prepositional phrases.

11. The technicians have made a grievous error, and now the dinosaurs have been set free.

12. He has a certain skill with customers, making them feel as if their every wish has been satisfied completely.

13. The dog looked longingly at the slab of raw meat.

14. If you want to invest your money safely, you should ensure you have a trustworthy broker.

15. My favorite album from last year was the third album from the Canadian band Arcade Fire.

16. My social studies report will hopefully be done by tomorrow morning.

17. Florida is the southernmost state of the continental United States.

18. School will likely be cancelled tomorrow due to inclement weather.

19. You should find the antique saltshaker on top of the fridge, behind the cereal boxes.

20. When will this dreary day ever end

Practice: Verb Tense/Form

1. Ophelia had already went to the game by the time we stopped by her house.

2. Trent and his sister had already set the table by the time their father arrives home.

3. The telephone had rang ten times before someone answered it.

4. In the kitchen, Alphonse slices the carrots, dices the beets, and simmered them all in a pot.

5. Even after he wrecked the car, Porter will insist that he is a careful and cautious driver.

6. After having rode all night to deliver the message, the young man felt exhausted.

7. Larry was horrified to find out that he had broke his wrist in three places.

8. Fiona does not like ice skating, because she will fear that she falls.

9. John already chosen the winner before they tallied the results.

10. The original design was changes after the head developer took a look at the plans.

For the next 10 questions, write the correct form of the verb in the blank.

11. The jacket was frayed and torn after he had _____ it for five years. (to wear)

12. Lissa _____ at school just before the bell rang. (to arrive)

13. Some students argue that playing video games _____ hand-eye coordination and problem-solving skills. (to improve)

14. Tomorrow, Pear Computers _____ its newest product: the mePhone. (to announce)

15. Jesse was disappointed when he found out the job position _____ two years of experience in the field. (to require)

16. The swimmer had _____ three laps before he realized that the race hadn't started yet. (to swim)

17. Crime psychologists believe that if a criminal feels true guilt, he or she _____ to turn themselves in. (to decide)

18. Pets require food and water, but they _____ hours of entertainment and companionship. (to provide)

19. The children were distracted by the class clown's antics and _____ the teacher's pleading for order. (to ignore)

20. Sarajevo is a classic example of a charming old-world city that was sadly _____ apart by war. (to tear)

Practice – Pronoun/Antecedent Agreement

1. The president's policies failed in part because it ignored the need to build international support through diplomacy.

_____

_____

2. The scientists are documenting the wolf's hunting patterns to determine whether it has changed since a new species of deer was introduced into the park.

_____

_____

3. The team realized too late that they were not prepared for the upcoming event.

_____

_____

4. Determined to lead a healthier lifestyle, Martin eliminated junk foods and meat from his diet and replaced it with natural foods like fruits, vegetables, and whole grain cereals.

_____

_____

5. Not one of the men in the room has indicated whether they would like to participate in the new project.

_____

_____

6. Each U.N. Security Council member has declared that they will support the new resolution authorizing the deployment of peacekeeping forces to the war-stricken region.

_____

_____

7. The boys collected all the booby traps they could find and, hoping to ensnare as many of the coming evening's dinner guests as possible, set it up in the various rooms of the house.

_____

_____

8. If one is going to write such a controversial piece, you must be prepared to deal with the intense criticism and debate that will likely ensue.

_____

_____

9. The orchestra members waited patiently for two hours for its conductor to arrive, but when he did not show up they went home.

_____

_____

10. When a stray alligator is picked up by the local animal patrol, they are taken to and detained at the nearest alligator pound.

_____

_____

Pronoun Case - Practice

1. Because of the recent rash of burglaries and other security breaches, the guards will no longer allow we students to enter the building after dark.

_____

_____

2. Before they go on tour next year, I would love to see she and Kevin perform some of their new song and dance routines.

_____

_____

C2 education
be smarter.

Unauthorized copying or reuse of any part of this page is illegal.

Version 1.3

3. Since this matter is one of grave importance to the future of the company, it concerns all top executives, including Harold and I.

_____

_____

4. Jack was trying to get the dehydrated dog out of the sun, so he quickly opened the door for she to come in.

_____

_____

5. Though Jack is the toughest fighter in the dojo, my friend Mark recently challenged he and his cronies to a day long karate tournament.

_____

_____

6. Feeling we had done enough studying for one night, Max and me went home to relax and get some sleep.

_____

_____

7. Between you and me, a major shake-up must take place within the administration in order for this school to pull itself out of the current crisis.

_____

_____

8. The principal asked that him and her shake hands and try to end their long-standing rivalry.

_____

_____

9. James considered how much trouble it would be to move himself and his brother Matthew into a new apartment and eventually decided that him and Matthew did not have the energy for such an undertaking.

_____

_____

10. For a while I was confused as to why everyone in the nursing home was suddenly catching the flu; then I remembered the feverish child that her and Jake had brought to visit their friend last Friday.

_____

_____

Yellow Grammar 9

Adjectives and Adverbs

Introduction

On the SAT, you may find a question that is incorrect because it uses an adjective where an adverb is called for, or vice versa.

 Example: Global warming would increase more (**gradual/gradually**) if solar energy sources were more fully exploited.

Can you tell which choice is correct? In this example, the correct choice is *gradually*. Gradually is an adverb. In this example, it was used to describe (modify) how global warming would increase. Increase is a verb and verbs are modified by adverbs. Adverbs may also be used to modify adjectives, and other adverbs.

 Example: We had to practice running up a (**gradual/gradually**) incline.

Was it easier to choose the correct answer in the second example? Gradual is the correct answer. In this example, gradual is an adjective and it describes the noun incline. As you may know, adjectives are used to modify nouns and other adjectives.

Let's review the differences between adjectives and adverbs.

Adverbs

An adverb modifies a verb, an adjective, or another adverb. Most, but not all, adverbs end in -ly.

 Example of an adverb modifying a verb:

The interviewer looked **approvingly** at the neatly dressed applicant.

Approvingly is an adverb that describes how the interviewer looked at the applicant. In this sentence *looked* is a verb.

Example of an adverb modifying an adjective:

He is a **truly** remarkable person.

Truly is an adverb that modifies remarkable. *Remarkable* is an adjective because it describes the person, a noun.

Example of an adverb modifying another adverb:

The group studies **very** diligently.

In this example, *very* is an adverb that modifies *diligently*. *Diligently* is also an adverb and it describes the verb *studies*.

Adjectives

An adjective modifies a noun or a pronoun.

Example: A woman in a **white** dress stood next to the **old** tree.

White is an adjective that describes the noun *dress*.

Old is an adjective that describes the noun *tree*.

Example: She was **happy** to have a **new** computer.

Happy is an adjective that describes the pronoun *she*.

New is an adjective that describes the noun *computer*.

Some adjectives end in -ly. Don't confuse them with adverbs. *Friendly, ugly, elderly, smelly,* and *lovely* are examples of adjectives that end in −ly. They are adjectives because they describe nouns.

Example: I have a **friendly** neighbor.

In this example, *friendly* modifies the noun *neighbor*.

Example: She wears **lovely** hats.

Lovely is an adjective that describes the noun *hats*.

Pronouns can be used as adjectives. *Those, these, this, that, your, my, our, his, her, its, each, all, some,* and *few* are examples of pronouns.

Examples of pronouns used as adjectives:

This flower…

That bowl…

His hat…

My shoes…

Exercise 1: Identify the Adjective

Directions: The sentences below are correct. As you read, pay attention to the correct usage of the adjectives. Underline the adjective in each sentence.

1. She was amazed by the exceptional beauty of the garden.

2. He sang a lovely solo at the concert.

3. Helen wore a purple hat to the wedding.

4. I bought an inexpensive blouse at the mall.

5. Winston ate the last donut.

6. Franklin wants more spaghetti.

7. Animals are amazing.

8. She seems happy.

9. Lottery winners are lucky.

10. Each flower is grown.

<u>Exercise 2: Identify the Adverb</u>

Directions: The sentences below are correct. As you read, pay attention to the correct usage of the adverbs. Underline the adverb in each sentence and circle the word that the adverb is modifying.

1. She desperately wanted a new car.

2. Anna happily accepted the offer.

3. Reluctantly, Lenny bought the ticket.

4. I was surprised to see him limping slightly.

5. Jamie found he was able to easily climb out the window.

6. They went inside.

7. Later, they walked to the park.

8. They quietly whispered in class.

9. We huddled together for warmth.

10. I was nearly ready for school.

11. Ken was completely surprised by the storm.

12. They wore very large hats to the party.

Exercise 3: Adjective or Adverb?

Directions: Underline the option that makes the sentence grammatically correct.

1. Eliminating (commercial/commercially) prepared sauces and seasonings is a good way to reduce the amount of sodium in your diet.

2. Although many people feel that parapsychology, the study of psychic phenomena, is completely frivolous, others take it very (serious/seriously).

3. Among the many problems facing the nation's schools today, the high dropout rate may be the (more/most) distressing.

4. The reading list for the course included short stories by five American authors, but most students found those by Poe (more/most) effective.

5. Archaeologists excavating the ancient Inca site removed soil very (slow/slowly) to protect any buried artifacts.

6. Although Delacroix is best known for the drama of his large canvases, many of his smaller works capture heroic themes just as (forceful/forcefully).

7. When movies were cheaper to produce than they are now, young directors were able to make films (easier/more easily).

Exercise 4: Adjective or Adverb?

Directions: As you read the following sentences, determine whether the underlined words are adjectives or adverbs. Write your answers on the lines below.

1. On Saturday, my friend and I <u>excitedly</u> hurried to the festival.

   _____

2. I <u>eagerly</u> anticipate the festival every year.

   _____

3. It is an opportunity to see <u>old</u> and <u>new</u> friends.

   _____

Version 1.3

4. I <u>always</u> ride the <u>towering</u> Ferris wheel.

_____

5. <u>Every</u> year, an <u>impressive</u> parade kicks off the festivities.

_____

6. There are <u>majestic</u> horses, <u>antique</u> cars, <u>festive</u> bands, and <u>many</u> people in the parade.

_____

7. I like all of the <u>delicious</u> food at the festival, <u>especially</u> the homemade pies.

_____

Exercise 5: Adjective and Adverb Errors

Directions: Correct the error in each sentence. If there is none, write "no error."

1. Though flawed in many ways, the film won the critics' approval because of its dynamic, realistic portrayed characters.

_____

_____

2. Whenever the neighborhood cat tries to sneak past the Jones's dog, it creeps slow and keeps its body low to the ground.

_____

_____

3. The director barked out orders so loud that some of the actors had to tell him to control the volume of his voice and be a bit more polite.

_____

_____

4. Since he had been studying steadily throughout the semester, Taylor finished reviewing for the biology exam rather quick.

_____

_____

5. Venetian glass factories are renowned throughout Europe for their exquisite manufactured glass products.

_____

_____

6. As the detective studied the area of the victim's final struggle careful, he thought he saw a piece of incriminating evidence.

_____

_____

7. George, searching desperate for a way out, scanned the hallway for the nearest exit sign or escape route.

_____

_____

8. After Dave's mother had tied his shoes tightly, the boy sprinted off with his friends to play on the jungle gym.

_____

_____

9. Glenn's partial torn hamstring will likely sideline him for the next several weeks and possibly for the remainder of the baseball season.

_____

_____

10. Greatly upset about his academic failures, Norton felt terribly about having to bring home his less-than-stellar report card.

_____

_____

11. Though many have claimed that it is an artistic superior production, the remake of the 1974 musical lacks the passion and authenticity of the original.

_____

_____

12. After being defeated quite thorough in the state finals, the Gators finally came to the conclusion that the other teams were simply more talented than they were.

_____

_____

13. The company's supervisors expressed concern about last week's shabby organized meeting, which probably turned off many prospective investors.

_____

_____

14. Despite signs of a possible mutiny, the captain's orders were dutiful carried out by the crew for the remainder of the voyage.

_____

_____

15. Organizing a meeting for the office staff requires an entire different set of skills than does writing a good financial report.

_____

_____

16. To the budding baker's dismay, the food critic scrunched up his nose and declared that the chocolate éclair tasted quite bitterly.

_____

_____

17. According to my brother, the mattress flew off the top of the car because we had not strapped it down secure before driving away.

_____

_____

18. The new Congress will likely applaud the President's radical altered foreign policy initiatives, which focus far more on diplomacy than on military action.

_____

_____

19. My classics professor claimed that the Romans were—by today's standards—quite bloodthirsty, notorious as they were for treating criminals, especially rebels, extremely brutal.

_____

_____

20. After the U.S. lifted the embargo against their country, many people there became quite hopeful that a more prosperous life awaited them.

_____

_____

Exercise 6: Adjective or Adverb?

Directions: Underline the correct answer.

1. We are going to grandma's house (late/later).

2. We will (happily/happy) celebrate the holiday with her.

3. She will teach us how to bake (deliciously/delicious) pies.

4. We will sing (festively/festive) songs while my cousins play instruments.

5. The big meal will be (completely/complete) devoured.

6. (Enthusiastic/Enthusiastically), the younger members of the family will play games.

7. Everyone will have (pleasant/pleasantly) memories of the holiday.

Exercise 7: Good vs. Well

Good is an adjective. It is used to describe a noun or pronoun. *Well* is an adverb. It is used to modify a verb, adjective, or another adverb. However, there is an exception. *Well* is used as an adjective when it is used to describe someone or something's health.

Directions: Underline the correct answer.

1. I am feeling (well/good) today.

2. She thought it was a really (well/good) movie.

3. Did you get (well/good) grades this year?

4. Because he was so (well/good) at basketball, he was invited to an elite training camp.

5. Do you think I play (well/good) enough to audition for the orchestra?

6. Did your friend provide (well/good) advice?

7. Did you do a (well/good) job of communicating during the interview?

8. Did you express yourself (well/good) during the interview?

9. He does not feel (well/good) enough to attend the party.

10. This is a (well/good) time to reevaluate your priorities.

11. Did you receive a (well/good) recommendation from your teacher?

12. The doctor says I'm (well/good) enough to return to school.

Exercise 8: Real vs. Really

Real is an adjective. It is used to describe a noun or pronoun. *Really* is an adverb. It is used to modify a verb, adjective, or another adverb.

Directions: Underline the correct answer.

1. Is this made with (real/really) cocoa?

2. Do you (real/really) believe what she told you?

3. I studied (real/really) well for this test.

4. He bought (real/really) diamonds for her.

5. She (real/really) wants to help others.

6. There is a (real/really) possibility that she could win the competition.

7. I heard a (real/really) good song on the radio today.

8. Is that plant (real/really) or fake?

9. Do you (real/really) have to leave now?

10. Don't you think he plays the piano (real/really) well?

11. I know that the Tooth Fairy is (real/really).

Exercise 9: Adjective and Adverb Errors

Directions: Correct the error in each sentence. If there is none, write "no error."

1. They spoke quiet in class.

   _____

2. I ran quick to the store.

   _____

3. The old car still runs good.

   _____

4. Do you feel good today?

   _____

5. Things are going good at work.

   _____

6. Be sure to dress appropriate for the wedding.

   _____

7. She painted the room a cheerfully color.

   _____

8. He sang beautiful.

   _____

9. He was real excited to see the horses.

_____

10. My team won the match easy.

_____

11. The speech was delivered very eloquent.

_____

12. They live on a desolately stretch of land.

_____

Homework: Adjectives and Adverbs

Directions: Write a story using at least half of the adjectives and adverbs listed below.

Adverbs

apprehensively	artificially	badly	deliberately	frantically	haphazardly
athletically	boldly	carefully	endlessly	fluently	helpfully
hopefully	impulsively	lately	lightly	neatly	well

Adjectives

good	jolly	calm	helpful	loud	real
bad	charming	splendid	stormy	adorable	unusual
proud	delightful	successful	crooked	inexpensive	cuddly

_____

_____

_____

_____

_____

_____

_____

_____

_____

_____

_____

_____

<u>Homework: Adjectives and Adverbs</u>

Directions: Correct the error in each sentence.

1. Since I am not feeling good, it will be difficult to accomplish everything on the list.

2. It wasn't a bad play, but it was poor performed.

3. Does your teacher have any well advice for you?

4. I can't believe he is real going to fly to Bangkok for business.

5. The stars appear to shine more brighter when viewed from a dark remote location.

6. She finished her exam quick and then met her friends for lunch.

7. The coach stood proud on the sidelines as her athlete won the race.

8. This stone wall is famous for its intricate designed carvings.

9. The snow fell soft on the ground.

_____

_____

10. If you are well at knitting, you can knit gifts for others.

_____

_____

11. Marchers wore festive decorated costumes in the parade.

_____

_____

12. He answered the question awkward because he was so nervous.

_____

_____

Yellow Grammar 10

Mixed Review

<u>Improving Sentences Practice</u>

Directions: The following sentences test correctness and effectiveness of expression. Part of each sentence or the entire sentence is underlined; beneath each sentence are five ways of phrasing the underlined material. Choice A repeats the original phrasing; the other four choices are different. If you think the original phrasing produces a better sentence than any of the alternatives, select choice A; if not, select one of the other choices.

1. James's ambition was <u>not only to study but also mastering</u> the craft of journalism.

(A) not only to study but also mastering

(B) not only studying but to try and master

(C) not studying only, but also mastering

(D) not only to study but also to master

(E) to study and as well to master

2. The Islandian government, under pressure to satisfy the needs of consumers, <u>and loosening its</u> control of the economy.

(A) and loosening its

(B) by loosening its

(C) is loosening their

(D) but loosening their

(E) is loosening its

3. To the surprise of the school's staff, the new freshman class at Ridgewood High <u>being larger than last year's</u>.

(A) being larger than last year's

(B) is large, most so than last year

(C) which is larger than the one last year

(D) is larger than last year's

(E) by far larger than the last

4. Night shift workers lead a strange life, working while the rest of us are sleeping, <u>then sleeping</u> while the rest of us are working.

(A) then sleeping

(B) after which they sleep

(C) then they sleep

(D) until they go to sleep

(E) but soon they are sleeping

5. <u>The young couple eventually returned to the grassy spot where they had left their sandwiches, strolling hand-in-hand.</u>

(A) The young couple eventually returned to the grassy spot where they had left their sandwiches, strolling hand-in-hand.

(B) Eventually, the young couple returned to the grassy spot where they had left their sandwiches, strolling hand-in-hand.

(C) Strolling hand-in-hand, the grassy spot where they had left their sandwiches was returned to by the young couple.

(D) The young couple, returning to the grassy spot where they had left their sandwiches, while strolling hand-in-hand.

(E) Strolling hand-in-hand, the young couple eventually returned to the grassy spot where they had left their sandwiches.

6. Amelia Earhart was born in Kansas the first person to fly from Hawaii to California.

(A) Amelia Earhart was born in Kansas the first person to fly from Hawaii to California.

(B) Amelia Earhart being the first person to fly from Hawaii to California and was born in Kansas.

(C) Being the first person to fly from Hawaii to California, Amelia Earhart was born in Kansas.

(D) Amelia Earhart was the first person to fly from Hawaii to California and was born in Kansas.

(E) Amelia Earhart, who was born in Kansas, was the first person to fly from Hawaii to California.

7. In the Middle Ages, when astronomical phenomena were poorly understood, the comets that seemed to portend military conflicts or other social crises.

(A) the comets that seemed to portend

(B) the comets seeming to portend

(C) the comets seemed to portend

(D) the comets apparently portending

(E) and the comets seemed the portend

8. Unusual numbers of playwrights and artists flourishing in the England of Shakespeare's time, and the Italy of Michelangelo's day, when cultural conditions were particularly conducive to creativity.

(A) flourishing in the England of Shakespeare's time

(B) by flourishing in the England of Shakespeare's time

(C) while flourishing in Shakespeare's England

(D) flourished in the England of Shakespeare's time

(E) having flourished in Shakespeare's England

9. During World War I, United States Army psychologists administered a forerunner of today's I.Q. tests, <u>where it had directions that</u> were given orally in acoustically-poor and crowded rooms.

(A) where it had directions that

(B) whereby there were directions that

(C) whose directions

(D) and for it they had directions which

(E) and it had directions which

10. A dispute arose between Rimland and Heartland over the eastern provinces from which twenty years before a great many people <u>had emigrated</u>.

(A) had emigrated

(B) emigrated

(C) had immigrated

(D) immigrated

(E) migrated

Identifying Sentence Errors Practice

Directions: The following sentences test your ability to recognize grammar and usage errors. Each sentence contains either a single error or no error at all. No sentence contains more than one error. The error, if there is one, will be underlined and lettered. If the sentence contains an error, select the letter of the incorrect portion. If the sentence is correct, select choice E.

1. The first female aviator <u>to cross</u> the English
                         A

Channel, Harriet Quimby <u>flown</u> <u>by monoplane</u>
                      B   C

from Dover, England, to Hardelot, France, <u>in</u>
                                  D

1912. <u>No Error</u>
     E

2. The reproductive behavior of sea horses <u>is no</u>
                             A

table <u>in respect of</u> the male, <u>who,</u> <u>instead of</u> the
        B   C   D

female, carries the fertilized eggs. <u>No error</u>
                               E

3. Early <u>experience</u> of racial discrimination <u>made</u>
         A   B

an <u>indelible</u> <u>impression</u> for the late Supreme
     C   D

Court Justice Thurgood Marshall. <u>No error</u>
                          E

4. <u>As long ago as</u> the twelfth century, French al-
     A

chemists <u>have</u> perfected techniques <u>for refining</u>
         B   C

precious metals <u>from</u> other ores. <u>No error</u>
           D   E

5. Galileo begged Rome's indulgence for his <u>sup</u>
                                   A

<u>port of</u> a Copernican system <u>in which</u> the Earth
                          B

circled the sun <u>instead of</u> <u>occupied</u> a central posi
               C   D

tion in the universe. <u>No Error</u>
                 E

Version 1.3

6. The chemist Sir Humphrey Davy was a friend

 of the poet William Wordsworth; he would visit
     A   B   C

with several other guests at a tiny cottage in the
                                   D

English Lake District. No Error
                       E

7. During the military coup, the deposed prime
    A

minister's property was put up for sale without
                       B

him having any opportunity to object. No Error
 C   D   E

8. The primary difference between the two posi
                     A

tions advertised is that one is exciting; the other,
             B   C   D

boring. No Error
        E

9. To conserve calories, to promote digestion, or
          A

so that they are less vulnerable to predators, wild
    B

animals rest during many of their waking hours.
       C   D

No Error
   E

10. It did not occur to the interviewer to ask
   A   B

either the job applicant nor his reference whether
                 C   D

the applicant had completed the project he initi

ated. No Error
    E

Improving Paragraphs Practice

Directions: Read each passage and select the best answers for the questions that follow. Some questions are about particular sentences or parts of sentences and ask you to improve sentence structure or word choice, while other questions ask you to consider organization and development.

Questions 1-5 are based on the following passage.

(1) Last summer I was fortunate enough to be able to spend a month in France. (2) It was the most exciting time of my life. (3) I stayed with a family in Montpellier, who were in the south of France. (4) It was very different from my life back in the United States. (5) Every morning we bought fresh bread from the bakery and had coffee in a bowl instead of a cup. (6) The milk came in bottles fresh from the dairy.

(7) Back home in Winnetka, Illinois, I wouldn't think anything of taking a ten-minute shower every day, or even twice a day in the summer. (8) In Montpellier, we only showered once every two days and were using far less water. (10) And it was pretty hot there in the summer, I'd never taken showers in cold water before! (11) I couldn't imagine what it was like in the winter. (12) I also noticed that although the family had a car, they hardly ever used it. (13) The father took the bus to work in the morning and the mother rode her bicycle when doing errands. (14) Since the family wasn't poor, they were well-off, I realized that gas is much more expensive in France than in the U.S. (15) I realized that as Americans, we can afford to take long showers and drive anywhere because we pay much less for energy. (16) Living in Montpellier and seeing how frugally people lived there, I get angry thinking of the resources wasted in the U.S. (18) I didn't drink coffee out of a bowl anymore, but I started riding my bike to school and turning the thermostat down at night.

1. In context, which of the following is the best way to revise sentence 3 (reproduced below)?

I stayed with a family in Montpellier, who were in the south of France.

(A) I stayed with a family in Montpellier, who were living in the south of France.

(B) I stayed with a family in Montpellier, which is in the south of France.

(C) In the south of France in Montpellier were living the family that I stayed with.

(D) The south of France in Montpellier is where I stayed with a family.

(E) I stayed in the south of France in Montpellier where lived in a family.

2. Which of the following sentences, if added after sentence 6, would best link the first paragraph with the rest of the essay?

(A) These differences were superficial, however; I was soon to discover other, more important ones.

(B) How I longed for my familiar existence back in the United States!

(C) I was not prepared for the culture shock I experienced.

(D) But I didn't let such minor inconveniences ruin my overseas experience.

(E) Although it took a while, eventually I got used to the new way of doing things.

3. In context, which of the following versions of sentences 8 (reproduced below) is best?

   In Montpellier, we only showered once every two days and were using far less water.

   (A) Showering only once every two days, Montpellier was where I used far less water.

   (B) Showering only once every two days and using far less water were things we did in Montpellier.

   (C) In Montpellier, we only showered once every two days and used far less water.

   (D) In Montpellier, where once every two days was when we showered, a lot less water was used.

   (E) In Montpellier, we were only showering once every two days and using far less water.

4. Which of the following best replaces the word *"And"* at the beginning of sentence 10 (reproduced below)?

   And it was pretty hot there in the summer, I'd never taken showers in cold water before!

   (A) But

   (B) Although

   (C) Yet

   (D) When

   (E) Which

5. In context, which is the best version of the underlined portion of sentence 14 (reproduced below)?

   Since the family wasn't poor, they were well-off, I realized that gas is much more expensive in France than in the U.S.

   (A) The family not being poor, they were well-off

   (B) Well-off, not poor, being the family

   (C) Since the family was well-off, they were not poor

   (D) The family wasn't poor but well-off

   (E) Since the family was well-off rather than poor

Homework

Identifying Sentence Errors

Read and answer the questions below. On the right-hand side of the paper, write what is wrong with the sentence in your own words.

1. <u>Because</u> I was seated on the dais <u>just</u> <u>in back of</u>
     A   B   C

the speaker, I could see the audience's <u>reaction to</u>
                                      D

his vituperative remarks. <u>No error</u>
                        E

2. A complete system of checks and balances

<u>have been incorporated</u> in <u>our</u> Constitution <u>from</u>
         A   B   C
 <u>inception</u> to protect the <u>principle</u> of equality.
                         D

<u>No error</u>
  E

3. <u>As a result of</u> the bad weather, she is the <u>only</u>
      A   B
 one of my friends <u>who</u> <u>plan</u> to attend the gradua
                   C   D

tion exercises. <u>No error</u>
                E

4. <u>Although</u> Mr. Jimenez <u>is</u> in this country <u>for</u>
      A   B   C
<u>only</u> two years, he talks <u>like</u> a native. <u>No error</u>
                    D   E

5. Every woman in the ward <u>fervently</u> hopes that
                               A

<u>their</u> child <u>will be</u> a normal and <u>healthy baby</u>.
  B   C   D
<u>No error</u>
  E

Improving Sentences

Read and answer the questions below. On the right-hand side of the paper, write what is wrong with the original sentence in your own words.

1. "Araby," along with several other stories from Joyce's *Dubliners*, <u>are going to be read</u> at Town Hall by noted Irish actor Brendan Coyle.

(A) are going to be read

(B) were going to be read

(C) are gone to be read

(D) is going to be read

(E) is gone to be read

2. In 1980 the Democrats <u>lost not only the executive branch, but also they lost the majority</u> in the United States Senate.

(A) lost not only the executive branch, but also they lost the majority

(B) lost not only the executive branch, but also the majority

(C) not only lost the executive branch, but also their majority

(D) lost the executive branch, but also their majority

(E) lost not only the executive branch, but their majority also

3. <u>Before considering an applicant for this job, he must have</u> a degree in electrical engineering as well as three years in the field.

(A) Before considering an applicant for this job, he must have

(B) Before considering an applicant for this job, he should have

(C) We will not consider an applicant for this job without

(D) To consider an applicant for this job, he must have

(E) We will not consider an applicant for this job if he does not have

4. <u>To invest intelligently for the future, mutual funds</u> provide an excellent opportunity for the average investor.

(A) To invest intelligently for the future, mutual funds

(B) As an intelligent investment for the future, mutual funds

(C) Investing intelligently for the future, mutual funds

(D) To invest with intelligence, mutual funds

(E) Having invested intelligently, you must determine that mutual funds

5. She was told to give the award <u>to whomever she thought</u> had contributed most to the welfare of the student body.

(A) to whomever she thought

(B) to whoever she thought

(C) to the senior whom she thought

(D) to whomever

(E) to him whom she thought

Improving Paragraphs

Read the short essay below. Use the lines provided to write 5 things that can be done to improve the essay. These things may include combining sentences, moving sentences, deleting sentences, or revising them.

(1) Though many people today live their life as they like, that is a relatively new phenomenon. (2) Over the years people have been oppressed in various ways. (3) The freedom to do what you want to do, say what you want to say, and be who you want to be is a rare and precious right. (4) History is filled with the people who have fought and died for this right.

(5) Have you ever heard of the Spanish Civil War? (6) The people of Spain were harshly repressed. (7) Conflicts between the government and Communist rebels bring Spain to a standstill. (8) The rebels, led by Francisco Franco, won the war in 1939. (9) Atrocities were committed by both sides. (10) After taking power, Franco was known for his harsh attacks against those who had opposed he. (11) Not until his death were freedoms restored. (12) This was in 1975 – over 40 years later!

(13) A more recent example would be South Africa. (14) This country separated its people by law. (15) The Europeans who had colonized this section of Africa created a system. (16) This system was called apartheid. (17) Under apartheid, people with different colored skin had different rights. (18) If you were white, you had more rights than someone who was black or had mixed ancestry. (19) This system was in place from 1948 to 1993. (20) They also freed a political prisoner, Nelson Mandela, who was elected president.

(21) The march of progress goes on. (22) Recently, many Arab countries have had major changes in their government. (23) As surely as the sun rises and sets, people will always fight tyranny. (24) Go people!

1. _____
   _____
   _____
   _____

2. _____
   _____
   _____
   _____

3. _____
   _____
   _____
   _____

4. _____
   _____
   _____
   _____

5. _____
   _____
   _____
   _____

Yellow Grammar 11

Coordination/Subordination

Constructing sentences is sometimes like assembling a puzzle. Each piece (or clause) must exactly fit with other pieces to make a full picture. If a sentence is not constructed properly, it will be grammatically incorrect and awkward to read.

Coordinating Sentences

>   Paul shopped for groceries, and Amy rented some movies.

In the sentence above, there are two ideas – Paul's errand and Amy's. (Each is an **independent clause** – an idea that can stand on its own as a sentence: Paul shopped for groceries. Amy rented some movies.) When you have two ideas in a sentence that are equally important, you should use a **coordinating conjunction**. (The coordinating conjunctions are *for, and, nor, but, or, yet,* and *so* – best remembered as the acronym FANBOYS.) These words connect two clauses without making one less important.

However, you must be sure to use the proper coordinating conjunction. Take a look at the sentence below:

>   Jared tried to buy a ticket for the game, *and* he didn't have enough money.

The problem is that "and" doesn't connect the two ideas in the correct way. "And" implies that these are two separate incidents. In fact, Jared's lack of money keeps him from buying a ticket. A better choice would be "but".

Exercise 1

Read the following sentences and determine if they are using the correct coordinating conjunction. If not, scratch out the offending conjunction and write a more fitting conjunction.

1. Alicia only met the man once, and she remembers him well.

2. The truck driver tried to pull out of the parking space, so his motor stalled.

3. Patrick got eggs at the store, yet he got bacon.

4. The directions on the box told him to use three eggs, and Zafar used six.

5. The casserole will be hot right out of the oven, but use some oven mitts to get it out.

Subordinating Sentences

Things get trickier when your sentences become complex. Remember, complex sentences have both independent clauses and dependent clauses. Dependent clauses are less important than independent clauses – sad but true. They act as support for the independent clause by providing additional information. Dependent clauses are created by using a subordinating conjunction – a list of which is provided below:

•After	• Although	•As if	• As though	•Because
•Before	•If	•In order to	•Since	•So that
•That	•Though	•Unless	•Until	•When
•Whenever	•Where	•Whereas	•Wherever	•Whether
•While				

These conjunctions, unlike their coordinating friends, make one clause support the other.

Version 1.3

Alan fell asleep during the test *because he had stayed up all night studying.*

In this sentence, "because he had stayed up all night studying" is the dependent clause. It gives us the reason that Alan fell asleep during the test.

Exercise 2

Combine each pair of sentences using a subordinating conjunction.

1. Alfred put on his glasses. He couldn't read without them.

2. Most people use cell phones. There are plenty of "land-line" phones in houses across America.

3. The neighborhood youths play hockey. The lake freezes over.

4. The laws will not change. New lawmakers are elected.

5. Reena changed into her pajamas. She went to bed.

Different subordinating conjunctions have different uses; some determine *time* (when, after, as soon as, whenever, while, before), or *place*: (where, wherever). Others may clarify the independent clause's *cause* (because, since, in order that, so that). Still others present a *contrast/concession* to/from the independent clause (although, as if, though, while) or *condition* (if, unless, provided, since, as long as).

Exercise 3

Read the sentences below and determine the use of each subordinate clause.

1. The doctor was prepped for surgery as soon as he arrived at the hospital.

2. Though he was intelligent, Caleb did too little work in his math class and failed the final.

3. The couple wanted to get married on the beach where the pavilion is located.

4. Matt and June can finish their project if they pick up their pace.

5. I'm not going to the movie tonight because I didn't get any sleep last night.

6. The old jalopy ran much better after we changed the oil and transmission fluid.

7. Unless the workers and management come to an agreement, the strike will continue into next week.

Subordination – Focus and Importance

An important thing to remember about subordination is that it changes the focus of the sentence. Look at the two sentences below:

> *Before they handcuffed him,* the policemen chased the criminal down.

> *After they chased him down,* the policemen handcuffed the criminal.

These two sentences tell the same story, but with different emphasis. In the first sentence, the emphasis is on the policemen chasing the criminal, but the second sentence makes the handcuffing more important. Using subordination properly can help express ideas more clearly; using it improperly can muddle a sentence badly. Look at the sentence below:

> When I saw my baby son for the first time, I was in the hospital.

This sentence is grammatically correct, but the logic of the subordination is questionable. Since "I was in the hospital" is the independent clause, it is implied to be the important part of the sentence. A much more logical version of this sentence would be

> When I was in the hospital, I saw my baby son for the first time.

Exercise 4

The SAT tests your ability to determine whether a sentence is properly coordinated or subordinated. Read the sentences below and determine if they are incorrectly written. If they are, determine how to fix them.

1. Although Francis practiced his violin every night, yet he was outperformed by Sonal.

2. Abraham Lincoln was born in Illinois, but he eventually became the President of the United States.

3. Lions sleep all day, they hunt at night.

4. Paris is a beautiful city, so it is never more beautiful than when it is lit up at night.

5. Before you boil the pasta, you mix the sauce.

6. I was looking down the street while I was hit by a car.

7. Portia successfully hiked the Appalachian Trail, although she had brought plenty of food and supplies.

Exercise 5

Now try these Improving Sentences questions about subordination and coordination.

1. Although her first business, a health food store, went bankrupt, <u>but she eventually launched a successful mail-order business</u>.

   (A) but she eventually launched a successful mail-order business

   (B) a successful mail-order business was eventually launched

   (C) and eventually launched a successful mail-order business

   (D) a successful mail-order business, successfully launched

   (E) she eventually launched a successful mail-order business

2. Because the carpenter would not do the work exactly as Edda wanted it done, <u>so she refused</u> to pay him.

   (A) so she refused

   (B) but she was refusing

   (C) she refused

   (D) and this led to her refusing

   (E) and she refused

Unauthorized copying or reuse of any part of this page is illegal.

Version 1.3

3. <u>Because her sons believed in the power of print advertising</u>, pictures of Lydia Pinkham appeared with her vegetable compound in newspapers across America in the late 19th century.

   (A) Because her sons believed in the power of print advertising

   (B) Her sons believed that print advertising was powerful

   (C) Being as her sons believed in the power of print advertising

   (D) That her sons believed in the power of print advertising, they put

   (E) Although her sons believed that print advertising was powerful

4. Yeats eventually created a unique voice in his <u>poetry, but he was</u> able to shake off the restricting influences of the British literary tradition.

   (A) poetry, but he was

   (B) poetry; however, he was

   (C) poetry because he was

   (D) poetry that was

   (E) poetry only while being

HOMEWORK

Read the paragraphs below. Then modify them by combining sentences in the best way you see fit. You may use coordinating or subordinating conjunctions.

1. Many chronic misspellers don't have time to master the rules of spelling. They might not have the desire. They may rely on dictionaries to catch their misspellings. Most dictionaries list words under their correct spellings. One kind of dictionary is designed for chronic misspellers. It lists each word under its common *mis*spellings. It then provides the correct spelling. It provides the definition.

   _____

   _____

   _____

   _____

   _____

   _____

2. Henry Hudson was an English explorer. He captained ships for the Dutch East India Company. On a voyage in 1610, he passed by Greenland. He sailed into a great bay in today's Northern Canada. He thought he and his sailors could stay there for the winter. The cold was terrible. Food was scarce. The sailors rose up against Hudson. They cast him adrift in a small boat. Eight others were also in the boat. Hudson and his companions perished.

   _____

   _____

   _____

   _____

   _____

   _____

   _____

Construct 6 grammatically correct and balanced sentences that each use a different coordinating conjunction. Underline the coordinating conjunction in each sentence.

1. _____

_____

2. _____

_____

3. _____

_____

4. _____

_____

5. _____

_____

6. _____

_____

Construct **5** sentences that reflect the factors for subordinating conjunctions. Underline each subordinating conjunction and, in parenthesis at the end of the sentence, indicate which factor was used (i.e., Time)

1. _____

_____

2. _____

_____

3. _____

_____

4. _____

_____

5. _____

_____

PRONOUN REVIEW!

Read the words below and correct any errors re: pronoun reference.

1. Though Dennis and Frank had both been witnesses, the court was interested in hearing only his testimony.

   _____

   _____

2. In today's <u>Washington Post</u>, they discussed the issue of ethnic unrest in western territories and the potential consequences such a conflict could have on the surrounding region.

   _____

   _____

3. In O.E. Rolvaag's novel <u>Giants in the Earth</u>, he depicts the hardships of prairie life in the 19th century Midwest.

   _____

   _____

4. <u>High Tech, High Touch</u>, John Naisbitt's third major book, describes the rise of computers and other technology and examines its impact on American society.

   _____

   _____

5. Mary used to go to church regularly to pray; these days, however, she has been avoiding it.

   _____

   _____

6. Having argued with my father and brother all day, I eventually gave up and accepted that I would never be able to overcome his stubbornness.

_____

_____

7. When I saw Allan and Mark walk into the market yesterday, he did not look content.

_____

_____

8. The fans shouted insults at him day after day; now, three months into the season, he can no longer tolerate them.

_____

_____

9. The head coach and her pitching coach, Mrs. Craig, were considered equally likely to be fired until she was rewarded with a contract extension.

_____

_____

10. Although Sheila is usually quite thoughtful and friendly, recently, perhaps because of her growing family problems, she has not shown it.

_____

_____

Yellow Grammar 12

Improving Paragraphs

The final – and shortest – part of the SAT writing multiple choice test is the Improving Paragraphs section. With only 5 or 6 questions in this section, it might seem like something to breeze through quickly, but in fact these last few questions require a little more work.

The section begins with a short essay – about two to four paragraphs, usually – with various errors and poor wording throughout. It is your job to fix this essay and make it presentable! After reading (or at least skimming) the passage, answer the questions that follow, which address those writing errors. Some of the tasks you'll be asked to do include combining sentences, revising sentences for clarification, and moving sentences around to improve the flow and organization of the essay.

While the improving sentences and identifying sentence errors sections ask questions mostly about grammar and usage, this section tends to be about the compositional aspects of writing: author purpose, organization and development of ideas, and relationships between sentences.

PROCESS

Step One: Before you read the essay, read the questions. This will give you an idea of which parts of the essay are the most important.

Step Two: Read the essay. You should pay particular attention to the passages that the questions ask about, but you'll still need to read the entire essay!

Step Three: Carefully – but quickly – answer each question. Reread the question, then look back to read the passage the question refers to. If you don't know the answer right away, use the process of elimination to narrow down your choices. Don't spend too much time on one question: If you just can't get the answer, move on!

APPROACHING THE ESSAY

When you read the essay, you should keep two important objectives in mind: determining what the writer is trying to say, and figuring out the best way to help him or her say it. This involves making changes here and there to the essay. The five to six questions will suggest these changes; your job is to pick the changes which will improve the essay the most.

Remember that the questions progress in the same order as the passage; thus, question 1 will be about the beginning of the passage, and the last question will be concerned with the end of the passage.

Read the essay below. In the space to the side, write what you think the essay's *main idea* is. Then underline any sentences that *distract* from that idea.

In order to help the author get across his or her point, the questions in this section ask you about three different things: general organization, revising sentences, and combining sentences.

GENERAL ORGANIZATION

General organization questions ask about how the essay works as a whole. Does this essay flow well? Does each sentence logically lead to the next? Should we add a line to the introduction? Take a look at this question about the short essay you just read:

Which of the following revisions would most improve the overall coherence of the essay?

A) Move sentence 11 to the first paragraph.

B) Remove sentence 22.

C) Move sentence 18 to the second paragraph.

D) Combine the first and second paragraphs.

E) Remove sentence 6.

Understanding the setup of the essay helps. The first paragraph is about finding the mess, the second paragraph is about figuring out how to fix it, and the final paragraph tells the story of how the narrator and her friends cleaned up the mess. Since each of the paragraphs is about a different subject, combining the first and second paragraphs would be unwise – thus, D is out. Both sentence 6 and sentence 22 are important to the essay's meaning as a whole, so we shouldn't remove either. That eliminates choices B and E. Meanwhile, sentence 11 would make no sense outside of the context of the second paragraph, as it's talking about the parks department. Sentence 18, however, doesn't quite fit In with the third paragraph; Mark's suggestion about contacting the senator sounds like something they'd do in paragraph 2. So choice C is our correct answer.

General organization questions not only require you to consider the essay as a whole, but also the author's intentions and technique for the essay. Look at this question, for example:

The author mentions the "internet petition" (line 16) for which reason?

A) To indicate the group's desperation for volunteers

B) To demonstrate new and useful ways to use the Internet

C) To show the variety of methods the group used

D) To warn against using internet postings

E) To add humor to the selection

So exactly why did the author mention the petition? If you look at the passage, the internet petition was one of several methods that the group used to gather a large crowd. (It was in addition to putting up posters and calling friends.) Thus, C is the closest to the author's intent. (Choice A is close – it does have to do with gathering volunteers, but nowhere in the essay do we see any evidence of desperation.)

Exercise 1 – General Organization Practice

Take a look at the essay below and answer the questions below.

(1) At the Battle of Gettysburg in July 1863, 75,000 Confederate troops faced 90,000 Union soldiers in one of the largest battles of the American Civil War. (2) For two days, both armies suffered heavy casualties in constant fighting, without either gaining a clear advantage. (3) On the third and final day of the battle, Confederate forces mounted one last effort to penetrate Union lines. (4) But the attempt ended in complete failure, forcing Confederate troops to withdraw to the south.

(5) Gettysburg was a turning point in the Civil War. (6) Before the battle, Confederate forces had defeated their Union counterparts in a string of major engagements. (7) After the battle, however, Union forces took the initiative, finally defeating the Confederacy less than two years later. (8) By invading Union territory, the Confederate leadership sought to shatter the Union's will to continue the war and to convince European nations to recognize the Confederacy as an independent nation.

1. Which sentence most appropriately follows sentence 8?

   (A) The Confederacy lost the war because it lacked the industrial capacity of the Union.

   (B) Gettysburg is considered by military experts to be the bloodiest battle of the Civil War.

   (C) France and Great Britain refused to provide the Confederacy with military assistance.

   (D) When President Lincoln issued the Emancipation Proclamation, which ended the slavery in the United States, the Confederacy's international position was weakened.

   (E) Instead, the Union's willingness to fight was strengthened and the Confederacy squandered its last chance for foreign support.

2. In the essay, the author does all of the following EXCEPT

   (A) describe a specific example

   (B) criticize an opposing viewpoint

   (C) explain the importance of an event

   (D) analyze the results of a historical event

   (E) discuss what happened on a particular day

REVISING SENTENCES

You might come across a sentence that is poorly worded, too complex, or just plain vague. (The SAT *hates* vagueness.) Revising Sentences questions give you the sentence and several different ways to rewrite it. In this way, these questions are much like questions from the Improving Sentences section; however, there is one important distinction. You must remember to take into account *how the sentence works in the essay.* This means you need to read a few lines above and below the sentence in order to make sure that whatever revision you make fits the essay. Many of these questions will have the words "in context" to remind you that the sentence you're fixing is part of a larger scheme.

Take a look at this Revising Sentences question from the recycling essay:

In context, what is a more clear revision of sentence 5 (reproduced below)?

(5) This wasn't the case.

A) Our plans to hike on that trail were foiled soon enough by the garbage deposited there by hikers.

B) We didn't have a good time, though.

C) Instead, our afternoon was ruined by other, messier hikers.

D) What we had expected, however, was not what we got.

E) The litter strewn across our path blocked our plan... and our path!

Saying "this wasn't the case" is a particularly vague thing to say; this question asks you to revise sentence 5 by making it clear what the writer intended with that sentence. Remember, we need to discover the context of this sentence before we decide on the best revision. Let's take a look at lines 4-6.

(4) We expected to enjoy our afternoon. (5) This wasn't the case. (6) When we got there, one could barely see the trail through all the trash dumped on it.

Looking at sentence 6, it looks like the trash on the trail is mentioned there, so we can eliminate E and A. (A is also too wordy, something else to look out for.) B and D are just as vague as the original sentence. That leaves C - our best answer. Note how the "instead" provides the transition from the author's expecting to enjoy the afternoon to the problems that come up afterwards.

Every so often, there will be a grammatical error in a sentence as well:

What is the best revision of sentence 6, reproduced below?

When we got there, one could barely see the trail *through* all the trash dumped on it.

(A) When we got there, one could barely see the trail through all the trash dumped on it.

(B) When those of us got there, we could barely see the trail.

(C) When one got there, one could barely see the trail through all the trash.

(D) When we got there, we could barely see the trail through all the trash dumped on it.

(E) When us got there, we could barely see the trail through all the trash

The big problem with this sentence is the pronoun shift from *we* to *one* – thus, D is the logical best answer.

And sometimes, you might just be asked to change part of the sentence:

What is the best revision of the underlined section of sentence 20, reproduced below?

(20) Three hours later, the trail was *pristinely clean and gorgeously beautiful*.

A) pristinely clean and gorgeously beautiful.

B) clean and beautiful.

C) pristinely beautiful.

D) gorgeously clean and pristinely beautiful.

E) clean.

Here, the sentence is too wordy – the phrases "pristinely clean" and "gorgeously beautiful" are redundant. It's like saying cleanly clean and beautifully beautiful. In this case, the best revision is B, which gets across the simple point that the trail was clean and beautiful.

Read these practice exercises and choose the best revision of each sentence.

Exercise 2 - Revising Sentences Practice

(1) Marine mammals like seals, sea lions, and whales would be in danger of freezing to death if not for their natural defenses against the cold. **(2)** Their principal defense consists of several types of insulation. **(3)** Body hair traps air, which is then heated by the body, creating a warm air mass around the animal. **(4)** More important than hair is a layer of body fat (or blubber) that lies between the skin and muscle. **(5)** Commonly known as blubber, it has a freezing temperature well below that of water. **(6)** Thus, it prevents the body's heat from flowing into colder surroundings.

1. In context, which is the best version of sentence 5 (reproduced below)?

    Commonly known as blubber, it has a freezing temperature well below that of water.

    (A) (As it is now)

    (B) Known as blubber, it has a freezing temperature well below that of water.

    (C) It has a freezing temperature well below that of water.

    (D) Water has a freezing temperature well below that of blubber.

    (E) The freezing temperature of blubber is well below that of water.

(1) The archaeopteryx, a prehistoric bird that lived in the Jurassic period 150 million years ago, is a perfect example of a transitional form in the evolution of modern birds from reptiles. **(2)** Despite its birdlike appearance, the bone structure of archaeopteryx suggests that it could not fly particularly well. **(3)** The absence of a sternum indicates that it had not fully developed the strong pectoral muscles that modern birds require for flight.

2. In context, which is the best version of the underlined part of sentence 2 (reproduced below)?

    Despite its birdlike appearance, the bone structure of archaeopteryx suggests that it could not fly particularly well.

    (A) (As it is now)

    (B) Because of its birdlike appearance

    (C) Due to its birdlike appearance

(D) In spite of archaeopteryx's birdlike appearance

(E) In contrast to its birdlike appearance

(1) The earliest colonists in America were not very concerned with creating a formal legal system. **(2)** Solutions to problems were based on common sense rather than abstract principles.   **(3)** Once England strengthened its hold over the American colonies, however, this informal system was gradually displaced by a formal legal system of laws, courts, and judges. **(4)** Even though it eventually rejected its political domination, its legal system rests heavily on the English model.

3. In context, which is the best version of the underlined part of sentence 4 (reproduced below)?

    Even though it eventually rejected its political domination, its legal system rests heavily on the English model.

    (A) (As it is now)

    (B) Despite its rejection of its political domination

    (C) Although America rejected its political domination

    (D) Its rejection of its political domination notwithstanding

    (E) Even though the United States eventually rejected English political domination

COMBINING SENTENCES

Occasionally, sentences in the essay will be too short and clunky. Read the following sentences and decide which of the two sounds better.

> "He walked outside. He shoveled the snow. He drove his car out of the driveway."

or

> "He walked outside, shoveled the snow, and then drove the car out of the driveway."

The second one flows more naturally, while the first is choppy and sounds awkward. Certain questions in this section will ask you for the best way to combine two, three, or even four sentences. You can't always string sentences together with "ands" and commas, though – you may need to use some subordination, as well. (Review lesson 11 for a refresher on coordination and subordination of sentences, if you need to.)

The sentences

"Frank has prepared extensively for this project. We should put him in charge of development."

Would best be combined this way:

"Because Frank has prepared extensively for this project, we should put him in charge of development."

There are many ways to combine sentences, some of them better than others. Like in the revising sentences questions, you will be given five different choices. You want to pick the one that is the most grammatically correct, the most concise, and the least confusing.

Here's a combining sentences question from the recycling essay:

What is the best way to combine sentences 7, 8, and 9 as reproduced below?

(7) We were so mad we couldn't even try to hike. (8) *We drove home.* (9) We discussed what to do about this.

A) We were so mad we couldn't even try to hike, drive home, and discuss what to do about this.

B) We were so mad we couldn't even try to hike, yet we drove home and discussed what to do about this.

C) So mad we couldn't even try to hike, we drove home to discuss what to do about this.

D) We were so mad that none of us could hike and subsequently we took a drive home to discuss what to do about this situation.

E) We drove home, so mad that we couldn't even hike, we discussed what to do about this.

First off, we can eliminate E, because it's a run-on sentence. Choice A doesn't work, because it makes the second and third sentences part of the 'try to' clause – meaning 'we were so mad we couldn't even try to drive home and discuss what to do'… and that changes the sentences' meaning. Choice B uses the conjunction "yet", which doesn't work well in the logic of the sentence. Choice D is too wordy – it even adds unnecessary words. Choice C is the shortest and best answer. It took the first sentence and made it into an adjective clause describing the subject ("So mad we couldn't even try to hike, we drove…") and connected the second two sentences by saying they drove home *to* discuss their options.

Combining Sentences Practice

Directions: Combine each pair of sentences into a single sentence that conforms to the rules of standard written English. Use the lines below the sentences to write your new sentence. There is no single correct way to combine the sentences. Just try to make your sentences concise and straight-forward.

1. Marsha went to the grocery store. At the grocery store, she bought cheese, eggs, and milk.

   _____

   _____

2. I attended a lecture at the university. My wife, on the other hand, decided to watch a movie.

   _____

   _____

3. Napoleon won many great military victories. Despite these military victories, he was eventually defeated and dethroned.

   _____

   _____

4. Interstellar travel is far beyond the limits of today's rockets. Their engines are not powerful enough to reach even the closest star.

   _____

   _____

5. The first function of tariffs is to protect local industry. And the second function of tariffs is to raise money for the national government.

_____

_____

Now that you've tried all the different types of questions, here is a quiz on the improving paragraphs section. Good luck!

Improving Paragraphs Practice Quiz

(1) When I was younger, I thought to myself, "Why do baseball players get paid so much for swinging a bat?" **(2)** Baseball, basketball, or football games they would have seemed like a real waste of money to me. **(3)** I would watch a game for about ten minutes without seeing a single hit and wonder why these athletes got so much money.

(4) I recently joined the Little-League home-team. **(5)** Before this time, sports was just recreation to me like wiffleball with my friends. **(6)** Once I began Little League, though, I went through all sorts of drills, like catch and batting practice. **(7)** I started to understand what it felt like to become an athlete. **(8)** Sure, natural talent helped. **(9)** I realized hard work and practice were just as important. **(10)** Because of my experience, I was able to appreciate professional sports more because I finally understood the strong commitment to the game that every professional athlete has to have.

(11) There is only a small group of great athletes. **(12)** Because of intense competition, hardly any of them in this group make it to the pros. **(13)** And the ones who want to make it have to dedicate all their energies to perfecting their skills so they can be the best. **(14)** People feel that professional athletes get paid too much for too little. **(15)** I'm convinced our sports heroes are receiving a fair salary for displaying and maintaining their hard-won skills.

1. Which of the following revisions of the underlined portion of sentence 2 (reproduced below) is clearest?

   Baseball, basketball, or football games they would have seemed like a real waste of money to me.

   (A) (As it is now)

   (B) Baseball, basketball, or football games seemed

   (C) Baseball, basketball, or football games will have seemed

   (D) Games of baseball, basketball, or football would have seemed

   (E) Games of baseball, basketball, or, football would be seeming

2. Which sentence listed below, if placed after sentence 3, would best tie in the in the first paragraph with the rest of the essay?

   (A) I have kept my point of view about the salaries of sports stars for a long time.

   (B) Still, my school coaches defended the excessive salaries of their favorite players.

   (C) My friends could never convince me to go to a local sporting event with them.

   (D) However, I ended up changing my mind about whether famous athletes deserve all the money they make.

   (E) Usually, sports personalities don't even work a full year.

3. Which of the following options is the best edit for the underlined portions of sentences 8 and 9 (reproduced below) so that the two sentences are combined into one?

   Sure, natural talent <u>helped. I realized</u> hard work and practice were just as important.

   (A) helped, and I realized

   (B) helped, so I realized

   (C) helped, so I was realizing

   (D) helped, but I realize

   (E) helped, but I realized

4. Which of the following words or phrases best replaces *And* at the beginning of sentence 13 (reproduced below)?

   And the ones who want to make it have to dedicate all their energies to perfecting their skills so they can be the best.

   (A) Therefore,

   (B) Besides this,

   (C) Nevertheless,

   (D) Moreover,

   (E) Including this,

5. In the context of the preceding paragraphs, which of the following would be the best way to combine the underlined portions of sentences 14 and 15 (reproduced below)?

   People feel that professional athletes get paid too much for too little. I'm convinced our sports heroes are receiving a fair salary for displaying and maintaining their hard-won skills.

   (A) While some people feel that professional athletes get paid too much for too little, I've been convinced that our sports heroes are receiving

   (B) In relation to people who feel that professional athletes get paid too much for too little, I will be convinced that they receive

   (C) Unlike some people, who feel that professional athletes get paid too much for too little, I'm now convinced our sports heroes are receiving

   (D) People feel that professional athletes get paid too much for too little and I am different because I'm convinced our sports heroes receive

   (E) People were feeling that professional athletes get paid too much for too little, I was convinced our sports heroes were receiving

6. All of the following strategies are used by the writer of the passage EXCEPT

   (A) referring to personal experience in order to illustrate an idea

   (B) quoting those whose opinions concur with his

   (C) using a narrative to develop a point

   (D) articulating a change of opinion from an original position stated in the first paragraph

   (E) supporting conclusions by evidence or example

(1) Recently a report came out in a science magazine that claimed the earth's protective ozone layer was being steadily depleted. **(2)** It named several companies that produced chemicals responsible for this situation, and consumers were advised by it to boycott these businesses. **(3)** An editorial in a business magazine insisted that this report was faulty. **(4)** It stated that there could be other, less dangerous reasons for the changes in climate that we've been experiencing. **(5)** However, I believe that the scientists are right, we should all consider the effect we can have on making sure the ozone layer is not harmed more than it already has been.

(6) In the past few decades, the ozone layer has been steadily depleted. **(7)** This means harmful ultraviolet rays get through to our atmosphere. **(8)** People who do these bad things which contribute to this situation should know that their actions could harm future generations. **(9)** Not buying products that are harmful to the ozone layer means our children's children will be more secure. **(10)** Consumers can choose to purchase any kind of product they desire. **(11)** They should be aware of what happens when they make their choices. **(12)** If they don't boycott companies that produce harmful substances, our atmosphere will steadily worsen.

7. Considering the essay as a whole, which is the best edit for the underlined section of sentence 2 (reproduced below)?

   It named several companies that produced chemicals responsible for this situation, and consumers were advised by it to boycott these businesses.

   (A) (As it is now)

   (B) It names several companies that produced chemicals responsible for this situation and advises consumers

   (C) Naming several companies that produce chemicals responsible for this situation, consumers are advised by the report

   (D) It is naming several companies that produce chemicals responsible for this situation and advising consumers

   (E) The report named several companies that produced chemicals responsible for this situation, and advised consumers

8. Considering the essay as a whole, which is the best way to edit and link the underlined portions of sentences 3 and 4 (reproduced below)?

   An editorial in a business magazine insisted that this report was faulty. It stated that there could be other, less dangerous reasons for the changes in climate that we've been experiencing.

   (A) The report was faulty, an editorial in a business magazine insisted, it stated

   (B) An editorial in a business magazine insisted that this report was faulty, stating

   (C) In an editorial in a business magazine was the insistence that the report was faulty and

   (D) The editorial in a business magazine insists that the consumers were faulty,

   (E) Insisting that the report was faulty, and editorial in a business magazine states

9. The phrase *do these bad things* in sentence 8 can be made clearer in relation to the content of the essay if it is edited as

   (A) exacerbate the situations

   (B) don't participate in events

   (C) are in need of services

   (D) use the types of chemicals

   (E) consider options

10. Which is the best version of the underlined portions of sentences 10 and 11 (reproduced below)?

   Consumers can choose to purchase any kind of product they desire. They should be aware of what happens when they make their choices.

   (A) (As it is now)

   (B) Evidently, consumers can choose to purchase any kind of product they desire. If they would just be aware

   (C) Consumers can definitely choose to purchase any kind of product they desire, in spite

   (D) Consumers can definitely choose to purchase any kind of product they desire, but they should be aware

   (E) While consumers can choose to purchase any kind of product they desire, they are also aware

11. Which of the following words or phrases best replaces the word *they* in sentence 12?

    (A) workers

    (B) future generations

    (C) consumers

    (D) chemical industries

    (E) editors

12. What sentence most clearly represents the main idea of the writer?

    (A) I understand now how the scientists who wrote the report are right.

    (B) From now on, consumers must refuse to buy products that threaten the ozone layer and the health and safety of us all.

    (C) In conclusion, we all have to watch out for each other

    (D) All of us have to find ways to maintain integrity in our economic choices.

    (E) Businesses are responsible for the safety of their products.

Yellow Grammar 13

Faulty Comparisons

One of the SAT's trickiest errors is the "faulty comparison" error. Sneakily, oh so sneakily, a sentence will compare two unlike things. These comparisons do not make logical sense, and thus are counted as an error. Read the sentence below:

Unlike the pelican, the talons of the eagle are sharp and can be used as weapons.

The two things being compared here – the pelican and the talons – are not at all similar. One is a bird, another is a body part. The comparison is illogical. We should compare the talons of one bird to the talons of another.

Unlike the pelican's talons, the talons of the eagle are sharp and can be used as weapons.

Or

Unlike those of the pelican, the talons of the eagle are sharp and can be used as weapons.

It may seem like a minor issue, but the SAT writing section sees it as an error. Thus, when reading a sentence, look to see if the sentence is *making a comparison*. Here are some words that indicate the sentence includes a comparison:

- ☐ like

- ☐ as

- ☐ less than

- ☐ more than

- ☐ compared to

If you see these words in a sentence, then your next step is to determine what exactly is being compared.

Exercise 1: Read the sentences below and determine which two things they are comparing. Underline the compared things.

1. Michael is more ambitious than Patrick.

2. The smell of pancakes in the morning is less pungent than the scent of the paper factory outside.

3. These scalped tickets were more expensive than the ones you bought at the ticket window.

4. Anna's enthusiasm for science often outshines the other students' enthusiasm.

5. Buying a new car with your money is a wiser move than spending it all on lottery tickets.

Remember that in order to be correct, the sentence must compare two SIMILAR things. Let's take a look at two incorrect sentences and determine why they're incorrect.

WRONG: The weather in Canada is colder than Mexico.

What's being compared here? Weather and Mexico. The concept of weather is in no way similar to the country south of the USA. What would a more fitting comparison be?

CORRECT: The weather in Canada is colder than **the weather in** Mexico.

Here's another one:

Martha's cookbook is better written than Mrs. Jones.

The compared items are "cookbook" and "Mrs. Jones." Can we really say that a woman is well-written? Certainly not in the same way a book is well-written.

CORRECT: Martha's cookbook is better written than Mrs. Jones's cookbook.

Exercise 2: Read the sentences below and determine if they make logical comparisons. If the comparison is illogical, rewrite the sentence with a logical comparison.

1. Our parents were aware that Frank's score on the test was higher than mine.

   _____

2. The shoes at DSW are more expensive than Foot Locker.

   _____

3. Healthy Greens brand lettuce is more nutritious than eating fast food.

   _____

4. Riding a bike in this weather is not as wise as a car ride.

   _____

5. The cinnamon rolls at this bakery are cheaper than the rolls at Windmill Time Bakery.

   _____

6. Visiting Paris, I noticed that its streets were cleaner and more beautiful than London.

   _____

7. Of the two patients, Patricia has a worse cough than Victoria.

   _____

Unauthorized copying or reuse of any part of this page is illegal.   Version 1.3

A poorly-written comparison can also confuse the meaning of the sentence.

> I like Maroon 5's music more than Lady Gaga.

This sentence could mean two things: you like listening to Maroon 5 more than you like listening to Lady Gaga, or you like Maroon 5 more than Lady Gaga does.

> BETTER: I like Maroon 5's music more than Lady Gaga's music.

Finally, a common comparison error occurs when you compare something to a group in which it belongs:

> Many fans of the band Pale Green Things believed that the group was better than any rock band.

If Pale Green Things is better than any band, then technically Pale Green Things is better than *itself*. After all, it's a band too.

> CORRECT: Many fans of the band Pale Green Things believed that the group was better than any **other** rock band.

Faulty comparisons are among the trickiest questions on the SAT, but with a little practice you'll find that they become easy to spot.

HOMEWORK

Write three sentences, each with a faulty comparison, on line A. On line B, write the corrected version of the sentence.

1. A: _____

   B: _____

2. A: _____

   B: _____

3. A: _____

   B: _____

Read the sentences below, and correct any comparisons that are faulty.

1. Like many politicians, the senator's promises sounded good but ultimately led to nothing.

   Rewrite:

   _____

   _____

2. As a manager and a problem solver, the governor was considered as creative as, or more creative than, writing and painting.

   Rewrite:

   _____

   _____

Unauthorized copying or reuse of any part of this page is illegal.

Version 1.3

3. Marine zoologists who have trained porpoises maintain that porpoises have powers of attention more sustained than chimpanzees.

    Rewrite:

    _____

    _____

4. The United States scientist's assumption, unlike Germany's Professor Heisenberg, was that the release of atomic energy would be sudden and violent.

    Rewrite:

    _____

    _____

5. Although some traditionalists still prefer typewriters to computers, most people agree that word processors are a great boon.

    Rewrite:

    _____

    _____

6. In the morning fog, Mount Hood looked more dramatically beautiful to us than any mountain.

    Rewrite:

    _____

    _____

7. The cost of a year at college these days is greater than a house was when my father was a boy.

    Rewrite:

    _____

    _____

8. According to some medievalists, women were treated with far greater respect during the Middle Ages than many countries in the 20th century.

Rewrite:

_____

_____

REVIEW: Adjectives and Adverbs

Remember, you need to look to see what the adjective (or adverb) is modifying; this will give you a good idea of which you should use.

> When asked about the recent scandal, the politician *careful avoided* making any remarks that could be taken the wrong way.

Look at that "careful." What is it talking about? It's not the politician. The politician avoided making remarks in a careful way. Since "avoided," a verb, is what "careful" is modifying, we should use the adverb "carefully."

> When asked about the recent scandal, the politician *carefully avoided* making any remarks that could be taken the wrong way.

Find and correct any adjective/adverb errors.

1. The wicked emperor was shocked to find that the band of heroes had foiled his careful laid plans.

   _____

2. Anna cheered exuberant when she found she'd been admitted to the college of her dreams.

   _____

3. Mark mentioned that the food in the garbage can was starting to smell quite pungently.

   _____

4. The quarterback, Luke Cafferty, mentioned that he was real excited to play the rival team in Friday's game.

   _____

5. The choir sang so beautiful that many in the audience were moved to tears.

_____

6. Zeena complained quite bitter about her broken pickle dish.

_____

7. Frank is doing good in his firefighter class and should graduate by next May.

_____

8. After the hike, we were all incredible exhausted and fell into our sleeping bags.

_____

9. Though he had often protested his innocence in the matter, Lou still felt guiltily about the incident.

_____

10. College freshmen find that the atmosphere at college is entire different from that in high school.

_____

Yellow Grammar 14

Mixed Practice

Improving Sentences

Directions: The following sentences test correctness and effectiveness of expression. Part of each sentence or the entire sentence is underlined; beneath each sentence are five ways of phrasing the underlined material. Choice **A** repeats the original phrasing; the other four choices are different. If you think the original phrasing produces a better sentence than any of the alternatives, select choice **A**; if not, select one of the other choices.

Practice Exercises:

1. This season the Raiders football games are mostly losses, <u>but those that do feature</u> considerable athletic performance.

   (A) but those that do feature

   (B) but they do feature

   (C) but that does feature

   (D) however featuring

   (E) however that does feature

2. Many of the students <u>studied relentless for passing</u> the test necessary to earn an A in the course.

   (A) studied relentless for passing

   (B) studied relentless to pass

   (C) studied to pass relentlessly

   (D) studied relentlessly for passing

   (E) studied relentlessly to pass

3. The violinist was overly excited at the beginning of the concert, <u>having shown admirable calm once the violin sonata got</u> underway.

(A) having shown admirable calm once the violin sonata got

(B) but he showed admirable calm once the violin sonata got

(C) but showing admirable calm once the violin sonata got

(D) once he showed admirable calm when the violin sonata got

(E) however, he showed admirable calm when the violin sonata had been

4. The compositions of modern composers and their <u>predecessors, suggestive</u> of Bach's later work in that beat, instrumentation, and style combine to form a very rhythmic sound.

(A) predecessors, suggestive

(B) predecessors are suggesting

(C) predecessors are suggestive

(D) predecessors suggesting

(E) predecessors, suggestions

5. Looking through the school's telescope on top of the science laboratory, <u>far above them a shooting star flew by</u>.

(A) far above them a shooting star flew by

(B) there was a shooting star flying above them

(C) a shooting star flew by far above them

(D) they saw a shooting star fly by far above them

(E) they saw far above them a shooting star flew

6. The increase in available space has made it possible for our library to be entertaining <u>as well as educate</u>.

    (A) as well as educate

    (B) and being educational as well

    (C) as well as educational

    (D) and educates as well

    (E) as well as education

7. In the mid to late 1500s, Queen Elizabeth I ascended the English throne and surprised much of English <u>society; she wanted</u> strong rule over her people and so did not marry.

    (A) society; she wanted

    (B) society, which allowed her to want

    (C) society, their idea was to want

    (D) society, and so she could want

    (E) society; in this way leading to the wanted

8. Whether there is truth to the assertion that there is extraterrestrial life in the universe remains unknown, <u>and somehow</u> many people have seen Unidentified Flying Objects (UFOs) in the sky.

    (A) and somehow

    (B) somehow

    (C) and that somehow

    (D) but somehow

    (E) that somehow

9. Because women buy approximately 80 percent of the ties sold in the United States, <u>they are often displayed</u> near the perfume or women's clothing departments.

    (A) they are often displayed

    (B) they are often in display

    (C) ties are often displayed

    (D) ties are often being displayed

    (E) they can often be found at or

10. Having read the works of Hemingway, Fitzgerald, and Steinbeck, <u>Hemingway is definitely over-rated as a writer</u>.

    (A) Hemingway is definitely overrated as a writer

    (B) Hemingway has definitely been overrated as a writer

    (C) I am convinced that Hemingway is overrated as a writer

    (D) the writing abilities of Hemingway are overrated, I am convinced

    (E) I am convinced as a writer that Hemingway is overrated

Identifying Sentence Errors

Directions: The following sentences test your ability to recognize grammar and usage errors. Each sentence contains either a single error or no error at all. No sentence contains more than one error. The error, if there is one, will be underlined and lettered. If the sentence contains an error, select the letter of the incorrect portion. If the sentence is correct, select choice **E**.

1. <u>One of the most</u> frequent types of injury that baseball players <u>sustain is</u> a dislocated <u>shoulder, an</u>
   ABC
   <u>other</u> that occurs <u>nearly as</u> frequently is a strained hamstring. <u>No error</u>
   DE

2. The hot-air balloonists <u>successfully traveled</u> around the world, but they refused to take full credit
   A
   either for the technology <u>they invented</u> for the flight <u>or for</u> their quick time, because they <u>had re</u>
   BCD
   ceived a good deal of help. <u>No error</u>
   E

3. <u>Although</u> she takes at least three singing lessons a week, Mary is <u>almost as</u> poor a singer <u>as she is a</u>
   ABC
   <u>dancer.</u> <u>No error</u>
   DE

4. Many international vacationers <u>find</u> airplane rides uncomfortable and <u>long, in</u> <u>other respects</u> they
   ABC
   enjoy <u>traveling to</u> foreign countries. <u>No error</u>
   DE

5. The relationships between identical twins <u>have a particular</u> fascination <u>for</u> many people <u>which</u> have
   ABC
   maintained close relationships with <u>their</u> own siblings. <u>No error</u>
   DE

6. <u>Exaggerating</u> <u>their</u> nutritional importance, <u>dieticians</u> overuse chocolate as an example of both a
   ABC
   <u>beneficial and a harmful</u> food. <u>No error</u>
   DE

7. Sam <u>liked</u> to read <u>novels;</u> <u>of which</u> he found mysteries <u>especially</u> gripping. <u>No error</u>
   ABCDE

8. Many <u>pieces of</u> music <u>composed by</u> nineteenth-century musicians in Europe, <u>in particular</u> religious
       A   B   C

    pieces, were <u>adaptations of</u> hymns sung in church. <u>No error</u>
                D   E

9. The <u>rapid spread</u> of infectious <u>diseases, frequently</u> compounded in certain regions <u>because</u> the
        A   B   C

    methods for detection and prevention are not <u>well understood</u>. <u>No error</u>
                                       D   E

10. Suzanne Farrell, a retired New York City Ballet principal dancer <u>widely known</u> for her grace and
                                                               A

    elegance <u>onstage</u>, <u>conducts</u> the <u>upcoming</u> workshop. <u>No error</u>
           B   C   D   E

Improving Paragraphs Practice

Directions: Read each passage and select the best answers for the questions that follow. Some questions are about particular sentences or parts of sentences and ask you to improve sentence structure or word choice, while other questions ask you to consider organization and development.

Questions 11-15 are based on the following passage.

(1) One of the most important achievements after the American Revolution was the creation of the presidential office. (2) This was difficult because they feared popular leadership. (3) In the Founding Fathers' view, it was dangerous for the President to gain power from popularity.

(4) The Founders believed in the ignorance of the populace. (5) The office of the President needed to be independent of the popular will and the "common man."

(6) George Washington was a perfect example. (7) Just as the Founders wished, his heroics and regal bearing put him on a pedestal. (8) However, some of America's most famous presidents did not follow the Founders' ideals. (9) Andrew Jackson (nicknamed "Old Hickory") identified himself as a "common man" and used his popularity as a military hero to win the presidential election. (10) In other words, he makes the presidency what it is today: a popularity contest.

(11) Fourteen years later, Abraham Lincoln was virtually everything the Founders had not wanted in a leader. (12) He did not stand above popular opinion. (13) He courted public favor as "Honest Abe." (14) He had humble roots, a fact that he emphasized to gain public favor. (15) The Founders would have hated this. (16) But many people think that Lincoln was one of our best Presidents. (17) This suggests maybe they were wrong.

11. Which of the following best replaces the word "they" in sentence 2 (reproduced below)?

This was difficult because they feared popular leadership.

(A) the revolutionaries

(B) the complications

(C) the Founding Fathers

(D) the Presidents

(E) the populace

12. In context, which of the following words are the most logical to insert at the beginning of sentence 5 (reproduced below)?

The office of the President needed to be independent of the popular will and the "common man."

 (A) I have found that

 (B) On the other hand

 (C) And yet, for him

 (D) To them,

 (E) Resulting in,

13. In context, which is the best way to combine sentences 6 and 7 (reproduced below)?

George Washington was a perfect example. Just as the Founders wished, his heroics and regal bearing put him on a pedestal.

 (A) (As it is now)

 (B) George Washington is a perfect example of what the Founders wanted although he was placed on a pedestal for his heroics and regal bearing.

 (C) Just like the Founders asked, George Washington's heroics and regal bearing put him on a pedestal.

 (D) George Washington is a perfect example of what the Founders wanted because his heroics and regal bearing put him on a pedestal.

 (E) George Washington is a perfect example of what they wanted, his heroics and regal bearing put him of a pedestal.

14. In context, which of the following revisions is necessary in sentence 10 (reproduced below)?

In other words, he makes the presidency what it is today: a popularity contest.

 (A) Replace "he" with "Jackson"

 (B) Replace "the presidency" with "the President"

 (C) Replace "it is" with "it was"

 (D) Replace "makes" with "had made"

 (E) Replace "makes" with "made"

15. In context, which is the best way to combine sentences 16 and 17 (reproduced below)?

But many people think that Lincoln was one of our best Presidents. This suggests maybe they were wrong.

(A) They were wrong, many people suggested, thinking Lincoln was one of our best Presidents.

(B) Suggesting that they were wrong, many people think that Lincoln was one of our best Presidents.

(C) But many people think that Lincoln was one of our best presidents, which suggests that maybe the Founders were wrong.

(D) Furthermore, many people think that Lincoln was one of our best Presidents, suggesting that maybe the Founders were wrong.

(E) Yet, maybe the Founders were wrong, many people think that Lincoln was one of our best Presidents.

Unauthorized copying or reuse of any part of this page is illegal.

Version 1.3

Homework

<u>Identifying Sentence Errors</u>

Read and answer the questions below. On the right-hand side of the paper, write what is wrong with the sentence in your own words.

1. Technological advances <u>can cause</u> factual data
               A
to become obsolete within a <u>short time</u>, <u>yet</u>,
                            B   C
students should concentrate on <u>reasoning skills</u>,
                               D
not facts. <u>No Error</u>
           E

2. <u>If</u> anyone cares <u>to join</u> me in this campaign,
   A   B
<u>either</u> now or in the near future, <u>they</u> will be
C   D
welcomed gratefully. <u>No Error</u>
                     E

3. The poems <u>with which</u> he occasionally <u>desired</u>
                  A   B
<u>to regale</u> the fashionable world were <u>invariable</u>
C   C
<u>bad</u>-stereotyped, bombastic, and <u>even ludicrous</u>.
D   D
<u>No Error</u>
E

4. <u>Ever since</u> the <u>quality of</u> teacher education
     A   B
came under public scrutiny, suggestions for

<u>upgrading</u> the profession <u>are abounding</u>.
C   D
<u>No Error</u>
E

5. <u>Contrary to</u> what had previously been report
     A
ed, the conditions <u>governing</u> the truce between
                   B
Libya and Chad <u>arranged by</u> the United Nations
               C
<u>has</u> not yet been revealed. <u>No Error</u>
D   E

Improving Sentences

Read and answer the questions below. On the right-hand side of the paper, write what is wrong with the original sentence in your own words.

1. We are more concerned that the best possible candidate be hired <u>than that one should follow bureaucratic affirmative action rules</u> to the letter.

(A) than that one should follow bureaucratic affirmative action rules

(B) and not about following bureaucratic affirmative action rules

(C) than that bureaucratic affirmative action rules be followed

(D) than your following bureaucratic affirmative action rules

(E) and not in any bureaucratic affirmative action rules being followed

2. <u>By the government failing to keep its pledges</u> will earn the distrust of all other nations in the alliance.

(A) By the government failing to keep its pledges

(B) Because the government failed to keep its pledges

(C) Since the government has failed to keep its pledges

(D) Failing to keep its government pledges

(E) If the government fails to keep its pledges, it

3. <u>Although I calculate that he will be here</u> any minute, I cannot wait much longer for him to arrive.

(A) Although I calculate that he will be here

(B) Although I reckon that he will be here

(C) Because I calculate that he will be here

(D) Although I am confident that he will be here

(E) Because I am confident that he will be here

4. Bernard Malamud was a forty-year-old college professor in <u>Oregon and his short story "The Magic Barrel"</u> was published in *The Partisan Review*.

(A) Oregon and his short story "The Magic Barrel"

(B) Oregon, his short story "The Magic Barrel"

(C) Oregon; his short story "The Magic Barrel"

(D) Oregon when his short story "The Magic Barrel"

(E) Oregon, furthermore, his short story "The Magic Barrel"

5. <u>Being as how a dangerous cloud of radiation was released</u> at the Chernobyl nuclear plant, that accident can be considered the most serious in the history of nuclear energy.

(A) Being as how a dangerous cloud of radiation was released

(B) Because a dangerous cloud of radiation was released

(C) Due to the release of a dangerous cloud of radiation

(D) In addition to a dangerous cloud of radiation being released

(E) Releasing a dangerous cloud of radiation

Improving Paragraphs

Read the short essay below. Use the lines provided to write 5 things that can be done to improve the essay. These things may include combining sentences, moving sentences, deleting sentences, or revising them.

(1) Today's world is connected more than ever before. (2) One can send photos of Stonehenge in England to your relatives in America in seconds. (3) This has led many people to call it "a smaller world." (4) But is it really? (5) While for some of us things are easier, this 'smaller world' excludes plenty.

(6) One thing you must remember is that while many people have technology, most don't. (7) In areas such as sub-Saharan Africa or the jungles of Borneo, things like wi-fi or internet access is nowhere to be found. (8) Even in developed areas, the luxuries we take for granted are simply not there. (9) Imagine trying to get Starbucks in a war zone! (10) Prosperity and connectivity are a relatively rare phenomenon. (11) Many smaller countries do not have the infrastructure to support technology. (12) Catching up to industrialized and highly-connected countries such as the United States could take billions of dollars for these countries. (13) In addition, those countries such as India or Afghanistan which are developing their infrastructure are often using corrosive or destructive materials. (14) Such as coal or crude oil. (15) Can countries like the United States or Britain tell these countries not to do this? (16) After all, they have been polluting the earth for hundreds of years by now.

(17) These are not problems that can be solved easily. (18) They cannot be solved quickly, either. (19) In conclusion, if we are trying to make it a smaller world, we should try to make it a more equal world as well

1. _____
_____

2. _____
_____

3. _____
_____

4. _____
_____

5. _____
_____

Yellow Grammar 15

Misplaced Modifiers

What is a modifier?

A **modifier** is a word or phrase that provides further information about another word or phrase. For example, an adjective is a modifier that tells you more about a noun ("the <u>shiny</u> badge"). An adverb is a modifier that tells you more about a verb, an adjective, or another adverb ("He <u>unhappily</u> sighed.").

Phrases can be modifiers. See below:

Hoping to catch the bus, David ran around the corner to see it disappearing from view.

"Hoping to catch the bus" is a modifier phrase that tells us about David: he's hoping to catch the bus. The most important rule you need to know about modifier phrases is this: <u>they should be near the object they are modifying.</u> Take a look at the same sentence, changed slightly:

Hoping to catch the bus, it disappeared from David's view as he ran around the corner.

The way the sentence is phrased implies that the bus was, in fact, hoping to catch itself. Take a look at another misplaced modifier:

The spices are in the cabinet which will be used in the sauce.

Unless this is some very strange sauce, the cabinet is not an ingredient: the spices are. The phrase "which will be used in the sauce" should be relocated, like so:

The spices *which will be used in the sauce* are in the cabinet.

Spotting these misplaced modifiers is an important skill to learn – these types of questions are

common in the Improving Sentences section. In order to understand these problems, you must first understand the different TYPES of modifying phrases. .

Appositives

Appositives are short phrases that further describe the subject of the sentence. They are usually set off from the rest of the sentence by commas.

☐ Shirley, **a mother of two**, loves to bake brownies.

☐ London, **the capital of England**, is a home of culture and bad food.

☐ My brother **Pete** is a master of ping-pong.

Prepositional phrases

Prepositions are all over the place in the English language. They are used to show relationships between things. Common prepositions include *about, above, across, after, against, along, among, around, as, at, before, behind, below, between, by, despite, during, except, for, from, in, inside, into, near, next, of, off, on, out, outside, over, past, since, through, unlike, until, up, upon, with, within,* and *without.*

Prepositional phrases, usually used as adjectives or adverbs, consist of a preposition and its object. (The object can be a noun, pronoun, or gerund.)

☐ The man *in the doorway* is waiting to come in. ("in the doorway" acts as an adjective, telling us more about the man)

☐ She was talking *about the new rules*. ("about the new rules" acts as an adverb, modifying "talking.")

Adjective clause

An adjective clause is a dependent clause that gives more information about a noun. These phrases begin with relative pronouns such as *who, which, that, when,* or *where.*

- The church *where my parents were married* is around the corner.

- The man *who gave us those tickets* is a boxing promoter.

- Socks *that come fresh from the dryer* are usually full of static.

- I still remember that time *when we snuck into the old construction site.*

Infinitive Phrase

An infinitive phrase consists of an **infinitive** — the root of the verb preceded by *to* — and any modifiers or complements associated with it. Infinitive phrases can act as adjectives, adverbs, and nouns.

- Her plan **to privatize Medicare** won wide acceptance among urban politicians. [modifies *plan*, functions as an adjective]

- She wanted **to raise taxes**. [noun-object of the sentence]

- **To watch Uncle Billy tell this story** is an eye-opening experience. [noun-subject of the sentence]

- Juan went to college **to study veterinary medicine**. [tells us *why* he <u>went</u>, so it's an adverb]

Participial phrase

A **participle** is a form of a verb that can be used as an adjective. There are present participles (usually ending in –ING) and past participles (ending in –ED or –D), both of which can become adjectives.

- The **startled** bird took flight. (The verb "startle" becomes the adjective "startled".)

- The poll had some **surprising** results. (The verb "surprise" becomes the adjective "surprising".)

A **participial phrase** uses a participle along with other modifiers (usually a prepositional phrase or a direct object). It acts as an adjective, modifying a noun.

- *Running through the fields*, the horse had never felt so free. (*Running through the fields* is an adjective describing the horse; "Running" is the participle, and "through the fields" is a prepositional phrase.)

- Mark sat silently, *eating his cornflakes*. (*Eating his cornflakes* acts as an adjective, describing Mark; "his cornflakes" is a direct object.)

Each of these phrases needs to be in its right place in the sentence. If a modifier is far away from what it is modifying, it may seem that the modifier is talking about something else.

INCORRECT: Sam found a letter in the mailbox that doesn't belong to her.

The adjective phrase "that doesn't belong to her" is out of place. It is talking about the letter, but it is placed near the noun "mailbox" – this implies that the mailbox doesn't belong to Sam!

CORRECT: Sam found a letter *that didn't belong to her* in the mailbox.

In order to clearly communicate the main point of the sentence, modifiers must be carefully placed.

Exercise 1 – Identifying Modifiers

Read the sentences below and identify which kind of modifier is underlined.

1. Sandra has always said that her greatest desire is <u>to get into Harvard</u>.

2. <u>Waiting for the bus</u>, Joe hoped he would not miss his interview.

3. Malik and his date planned to meet <u>at the movie theater.</u>

4. The dance sensation <u>that is sweeping the nation</u> is called the Frug.

5. <u>On Saturday</u>, the coach reviewed the tapes of last night's football game.

6. The pond, <u>frozen over since early December</u>, is now safe for ice-skating.

7. *Anna Karenina*, <u>one of the most famous Russian novels</u>, tells the story of a society woman's affair.

8. Tommy scrubbed the tile floor <u>until his arms ached</u>.

Exercise 2 – Moving Modifiers

Read the sentences below. The modifier in each sentence is in the wrong place. Draw a box around the modifier and an arrow pointing where the modifier should go.

The box was given to the homeless man full of blankets.

1. The young man waited at the train station wearing glasses.

2. Edmund Spenser wrote The Fairie Queene, a famous poet from the 1600s.

3. The dog chased the boy wearing a spiked collar.

4. Running across the room, the rug slipped when I lost my balance.

5. They bought a puppy for my brother that was named Spot.

6. The patient was examined by the doctor with a gaping wound.

7. She could not explain why she wanted to get married to her mother.

8. Stopping to catch his breath, the cab flew by Jason and he missed it.

Exercise 3 – Rephrasing Sentences

Read the sentences below. Rewrite them with the modifiers in their correct place.

1. They reported that Giuseppe Balle, a European rock star, had died on the six o'clock news.

   _____

2. For sale: An antique desk suitable for a lady with thick legs and large drawers.

   _____

3. Adriana wrote that her father had died in her last letter.

   _____

4. Breathing heavily, a mile was run by Jason in 8 minutes.

   _____

5. An order was sent out by a colonel with dreams of promotion to clean the latrines.

   _____

6. Two cars were reported stolen by the police yesterday.

   _____

7. Barking loudly, Willa couldn't get to sleep because of the neighbor's dog.

_____

8. The vines of ivy were trimmed by the gardener climbing up the wall.

_____

Homework

Exercise 1

Read the sentences below. Underline the word which is being modified by the sentence's modifying phrase (given in italics).

1. Eric grimaced *when he saw the messy apartment.*

2. I gave the teddy bear *that I'd owned since childhood* to my nephew.

3. The setting *of the sun* never fails to bring a tear to the old butler's eye.

4. Jamal finished his run, *gasping for breath.*

5. The teacher's strict rules prevent us *from talking in class.*

6. Studying nightly is incredibly important if you want *to succeed in school.*

Exercise 2

These sentences are Improving Sentences questions from an actual SAT. Choose the answer that best changes the sentence so that the modifiers are close to what they modify.

1. <u>A familiar marketing strategy was reintroduced by a former client that</u> had served the company dependably in the past.

   (A) A familiar marketing strategy was reintroduced by a former client that

   (B) By reintroducing a familiar marketing strategy, the former client that

   (C) Reintroduced by a former client, a familiar marketing strategy that

   (D) A former client reintroduced a familiar marketing strategy that

   (E) A former client, by reintroducing a familiar marketing strategy

2. <u>After practicing for months, auditions went much more smoothly for the young actor.</u>

   (A) After practicing for months, auditions went much more smoothly for the young actor.

   (B) Auditions, after practicing for months, went much more smoothly for the young actor.

   (C) The young actor having practiced for auditions for months, auditions went much more smoothly for him.

   (D) The young actor presenting auditions after months of practice, they went much more smoothly.

   (E) The young actor presented auditions much more smoothly after practicing for months.

3. To ensure that a novel will sell well, <u>it should appeal to currently popular tastes</u>.

   (A) it should appeal to currently popular tastes

   (B) a novel should be appealing to currently popular tastes

   (C) a writer should appeal to currently popular tastes

   (D) currently popular tastes should be appealed to

   (E) currently popular tastes should be appealed to by the novel

4. Hoping to receive a promotion, <u>the letter he received instead informed the employee</u> that he had been fired.

   (A) the letter he received instead informed the employee

   (B) the letter having been received, instead informing the employee

   (C) the employee instead received a letter informing him

   (D) information from the received letter instead told the employee

   (E) the employee, instead informed by the letter he received

5. <u>A cornerstone of the community since 1925, the fund-raising drive did not generate enough revenue to keep the recreational center operating another year.</u>

(A) A cornerstone of the community since 1925, the fund-raising drive did not generate enough revenue to keep the recreational center operating another year.

(B) The fund-raising drive did not generate enough revenue to keep the recreational center, a cornerstone of the community since 1925, operating another year.

(C) The fund-raising drive did not generate enough revenue, a cornerstone of the community since 1925, to keep the recreational center operating another year.

(D) A cornerstone of the community since 1925, the recreational center did not generate enough revenue to keep the fund-raising drive operating another year.

(E) The fund-raising drive, a cornerstone of the community since 1925, did not generate enough revenue to keep the recreational center operating another year.

On the lines below, write two sentences using each of the modifiers discussed in this lesson.

Appositive

1)_____

2)_____

Adjective Phrase

1)_____

2)_____

Infinitive Phrase

1)_____

2)_____

Unauthorized copying or reuse of any part of this page is illegal.

Version 1.3

Prepositional Phrase

1) _____

2) _____

Participial Phrase

1) _____

2) _____

Yellow Grammar 16

Wordiness

Introduction

In writing and speech, it is important to edit sentences to remove unnecessary words. Sentences should be as concise as possible. Unnecessary words repeat something that was already said or implied.

Some SAT problems test your ability to spot sentences that are too wordy. These problems will include several sentences that contain unnecessary words and one that is written concisely. You will have to choose the correct sentence, making sure that your answer does not include any redundant ideas, words, or phrases.

Consider the following sample problems.

Sample 1

In this day and age in which we live, there are too many people who do not value education and believe in a good education and learning.

   A. In this day and age in which we live, there are too many people who do not value and believe in education and learning.

   B. In this day and age, there are too many people who do not believe in a good education and learning.

   C. In this day and age in which we live, there are many people who do not believe in a good education.

   D. Today, there are many people who do not believe in education.

   E. Today, many people do not value education.

Choice E is the correct answer. It eliminates the phrase "in this day and age," which is a redundant phrase because day and age mean the same thing in this context. "In which we live" is a redundant phrase because we live in the present, not in the past or future. The phrase "too many people" can be replaced with "many people." "Value" and "believe in" mean the same thing in this context, and the word value is preferred because it is a single word. The phrase "Education and learning" can be replaced with the word "education" because learning is implied. People could even be taken out of the sentence because "many" implies people in this context.

Version 1.3

Sample 2

We don't want to have to go to school during the summer and winter breaks when we are not in school, and don't think the school year should be extended.

   A. We don't want to have to go to school during the summer and winter breaks when we are not in school, and don't think the school year should be extended.

   B. We don't want to go to school during the summer and winter breaks and do not think the school year should be extended.

   C. We don't think the school year should be extended.

   D. We don't want the school year to be extended during the breaks.

   E. We don't want to go to school during the breaks and do not think the school year should be extended.

     Choice C is the correct answer. It offers the most concise statement of the main idea that any change in the school year that increases the number of class days at the expense of time off would be considered undesirable.

Exercise 1

Choose the best (least wordy) sentence.

1. What I'm meaning to say is that I think cherry pie is the best kind of pie, especially when it is homemade.

   A. What I'm meaning to say is that I think cherry pie is the best kind of pie, especially when it is homemade.

   B. What I'm meaning to say is that I think homemade cherry pie is the best type of pie.

   C. I think homemade cherry pie is best.

   D. What I think is that homemade cherry pie is best.

2. Everyone thinks I'm a naturally talented musician, but the fact of the matter is that I have to practice diligently every day of the year.

   A. Everyone thinks I'm a naturally talented musician, but the fact of the matter is that I have to practice diligently every day of the year.

   B. Everyone thinks I'm a naturally talented musician, but I have to practice diligently every day of the year.

   C. Everyone thinks I'm a naturally talented musician, but I have to practice diligently every day.

   D. Everyone thinks I'm a naturally talented musician, but the fact of the matter is that I have to practice every day.

3. I need to go to the bookstore today because I want to buy a birthday present for my sister.

   A. I need to go to the bookstore today because I want to buy a birthday present for my sister.

   B. I need to go to the bookstore today, and the reason why is because I want to buy a birthday present for my sister.

   C. I need to go to the bookstore today because I want to buy a present for my sister for her birthday.

   D. I need to go to the bookstore today and reason why is to buy a present for my sister for her birthday.

4. I want to be a marine biologist when I grow up on account of how I like to study marine life when I go scuba diving in the ocean.

   A. I want to be a marine biologist when I grow up on account of how I like to study marine life when I go scuba diving in the ocean.

   B. I want to be a marine biologist because I like to study marine life when I go scuba diving.

   C. I want to be a marine biologist on account of how I like to study marine life when I go scuba diving.

   D. I want to be a marine biologist when I grow up because I like to study marine life when I go scuba diving.

5. My mother is of the belief that if I go outside with my hair wet I will catch a cold and get sick.

   A. My mother is of the belief that if I go outside with my hair wet I will catch a cold.

   B. My mother believes that if I go outside with my hair wet I will catch a cold and get sick.

   C. My mother is of the belief that I will catch a cold and get sick if I go outside with my hair wet.

   D. My mother believes that I will catch a cold if I go outside with my hair wet.

6. In spite of the fact that Carl does not like spiders, he climbed up into the attic anyway because he wanted to try to find his favorite glove for baseball.

   A. In spite of the fact that Carl does not like spiders, he climbed up into the attic because he wanted to find his favorite glove for baseball.

   B. Although Carl does not like spiders, he climbed up into the attic anyway because he wanted to try to find his favorite glove for baseball.

   C. Although Carl does not like spiders, he climbed into the attic anyway because he wanted to find his favorite baseball glove.

   D. In spite of the fact that Carl does not like spiders, he climbed up into the attic because he wanted to find his favorite baseball glove.

7. This food puts me in mind of cooking my grandmother used to make for me.

   A. This food puts me in mind of cooking my grandmother used to make.

   B. This food reminds me of cooking my grandmother used to make for me.

   C. This food puts me in a mind of my grandmother's cooking.

   D. This food reminds me of my grandmother's cooking.

Exercise 2

In this exercise, part of each sentence is underlined. Beneath each sentence are five ways of phrasing the underlined material. Choice **A** repeats the original phrasing; the other four choices are different. If you think the original phrasing produces a better sentence than any of the alternatives, select choice **A**; if not, select one of the other choices.

1. Jason's article was pulled from the weekly paper because it claimed <u>not only that he was not being compensated fairly but the paper's editors were holding a grudge against him</u>.

   A. not only that he was not being compensated fairly but the paper's editors were holding a grudge against him

   B. not only that he was not being compensated fairly and also the paper's editors were holding a grudge against him as well

   C. that he was not being compensated fairly but in addition that the paper's editors were holding a grudge against him as well

   D. that he was not being compensated fairly and that the paper's editors were holding a grudge against him

   E. that he was not being compensated fairly and he also believed that the paper's editors were holding a grudge against him

2. To be eligible for the junior swim team, a student should be able both to tread water for five minutes <u>and her exhaling when underwater should be normal</u>.

   A. and her exhaling when underwater should be normal

   B. while her exhaling underwater is normal

   C. and her exhaling underwater being normal

   D. with exhaling normally underwater

   E. and to exhale normally underwater

Unauthorized copying or reuse of any part of this page is illegal.

Version 1.3

3. Vision loss caused by a head injury often lasts for only a few days, <u>and this is not true of vision loss caused by a progressive disease, which is often</u> permanent.

    A. and this is not true of vision loss caused by a progressive disease, which is often

    B. not true of vision loss caused by a progressive disease, which is often

    C. as opposed to vision loss caused by a progressive disease

    D. vision loss caused by a progressive disease being often

    E. but vision loss caused by a progressive disease is often

4. Although he claimed to have considered each interview candidate equally, <u>Brian based his choice on the candidates' qualifications less than what he did on</u> their business connections.

    A. Brian based his choice on the candidates' qualifications less than what he did on

    B. Brian's choice is based less on the candidates' qualifications than it was on

    C. Brian based his choice less on the candidates' qualifications than on

    D. Brian made his choice, and this choice being based less on the candidates' qualifications than on

    E. Brian making a choice based on the candidates' qualifications less than

Exercise 3

The sentences below are too wordy. Think about how the same meaning could be conveyed in a more concise manner. Write your corrected version of the sentence on the line provided.

1. During this past summer break from school, I visited an amusement park that is only open during the summer.

_____

_____

_____

2. I went to the amusement park with my family, including my father, mother, and sister.

_____

_____

_____

3. When we arrived at the park, we had to drive around the parking lot for a long time looking for a parking space which was difficult to find since there were already so many cars there.

_____

_____

_____

4. We walked a long way across the parking lot, which as hot because it was a sunny day, and then stopped at the front gate of the amusement park.

_____

_____

_____

5. We bought tickets at the ticket counter and then we walked through the gate and we were finally inside the amusement park!

_____

_____

_____

6. The first thing we did was we walked to the best ride in the park which is the most popular ride.

_____

_____

_____

7. Due to the fact that my dad is afraid of heights, he did not go on some of the rides with us.

_____

_____

_____

8. Later in the day, we all went to a pizza place inside the park and ate pizza for lunch.

_____

_____

_____

9. During the hot afternoon, while it was really hot outside, we went to the water park to cool off in the water.

_____

_____

_____

10. In spite of the fact that dad is afraid of heights, he likes the water rides because they are not as tall and do not go as fast as roller coaster rides.

_____

_____

_____

11. All in all, it was a very fun day at the amusement park.

_____

_____

_____

12. In this day and age, I think it is important to set aside days to have fun like we did at the amusement park.

_____

_____

_____

Exercise 4

The following sentences were hastily written and need to be revised. Read each sentence and think about how it could be rewritten to convey the same information in a more concise manner. Write your corrected version of the sentence on the line provided.

1. In eleventh grade, when I was a junior in high school, my friend and I went on a trip together to Washington, D.C., the nation's capital.

_____

_____

_____

2. It was the first time I was on an airplane and it was the first time my friend was on an airplane, too.

_____

_____

_____

3. The flight attendant gave us each a pin to wear and the pin had little wings on it.

_____

_____

_____

 **C2 education** be smarter.

Unauthorized copying or reuse of any part of this page is illegal.

Version 1.3

4. It was very exciting and exhilarating when the plane started to move and started to take off.

    _____

    _____

    _____

5. Once the plane started to climb higher and higher, my ears became very plugged up and I couldn't hear my friend when he tried to talk to me.

    _____

    _____

    _____

6. My friend gave me a piece of chewing gum and I chewed the gum and then my ears unplugged and I could hear again.

    _____

    _____

    _____

7. Soon, we were very high in the sky and we wanted to see the views so we crowded together side by side at the window and looked out the window at the view.

    _____

    _____

    _____

8. The clouds and the bright sunshine looked so beautiful and the city below looked so beautiful.

    _____

    _____

    _____

9. The cars looked like miniature cars and the buildings looked like miniature buildings too.

_____

_____

_____

10. Next we flew over mountains and it was amazing to get a bird's eye view of the mountain range.

_____

_____

_____

11. During the middle of the flight the flight attendant came to see us to check on us and see if we were in need of anything.

_____

_____

_____

12. I ordered soda because I was thirsty and my friend ordered soda, too.

_____

_____

_____

13. The flight was fairly short and didn't last for very long at all.

_____

_____

_____

Unauthorized copying or reuse of any part of this page is illegal.

Version 1.3

14. Finally, the plane started its descent and as it descended I was a little sad that my first plane ride was almost at an end.

_____

_____

_____

15. As soon as we landed, however, I was excited as I was very elated to start my next adventure, which was to get to see Washington, D.C.

_____

_____

_____

Exercise 5

Pretend that the story below was written by a classmate for your group project. Your other teammate has already proofread the story and underlined some areas that are too wordy and need to be revised. However, the classmate did not catch every mistake. There are two things she missed. Since you are the second proofreader, read the story and underline the two additional problems. Then, consider how each underlined problem could be rewritten in a more concise manner. Finally, write your corrected version of the story on the lines provided.

Once upon a time there lived <u>a princess and this princess was</u> in search of a prince. She searched <u>far and wide, near and far</u>, and was almost ready to give up. Then, her trusty assistant told her to stop looking <u>for the perfect prince of her dreams and only existed in her dreams</u>. This seemed like good advice, she reluctantly admitted, <u>and so she took the advice to heart</u>. The princess sent her assistants out with orders to expand their search for a suitable candidate.

The first assistant searched around the tranquil pond, but, alas, only found frogs. The second assistant searched the tall peaks of the highest mountain range and only found mountain goats in the mountains. The third assistant scoured the forest but only found chipmunks <u>in the forest</u>. The fourth assistant explored the seashore and only found fish.

The princess grew restless with the poor results and decided to go out for a while to clear her mind <u>so she could think</u>. She wandered along the beautiful, tranquil, <u>peaceful</u>, emerald fields overlooking the sea. <u>In the emerald fields</u> she ran into the oldest, wisest, person in the kingdom.

"Good morning, Princess." The wise elder addressed her in <u>the usual customary royal</u> fashion.

"It's a pleasure to meet you, Wise Elder. Many speak highly of you," the Princess replied.

"Princess, <u>you look as if you could be in need of some useful</u> guidance," the Wise Elder kindly offered.

"Yes, thank you," the Princess replied, sounding relieved. "Please <u>tell me as to how I will ever find a prince</u>. <u>Despite the fact that</u> my assistants have searched <u>far and wide, high and low</u>, they have found <u>no one to be my prince</u>. Please <u>offer me some piece of advice</u>, Wise Elder."

"Yes, I will be happy to. I believe you will find your prince." The wise elder smiled.

_____

_____

_____

_____

_____

_____

_____

_____

_____

_____

_____

Homework: Wordiness

In this exercise, part of each sentence is underlined. Beneath each sentence are five ways of phrasing the underlined material. Choice **A** repeats the original phrasing; the other four choices are different. If you think the original phrasing produces a better sentence than any of the alternatives, select choice **A**; if not, select one of the other choices.

1. <u>Time and time again, Jen has repeatedly</u> offered to help me with my homework.

   A. Time and time again, Jen has repeatedly

   B. Time and time again, Jen has

   C. Jen has repeatedly

   D. Many times, Jen has repeatedly

2. I have <u>practiced this passage over and over again</u> in order to perfect my speech.

   A. practiced this passage over and over again

   B. practiced this passage again and again

   C. practiced this passage time and time again

   D. repeatedly practiced this passage

3. <u>In this day and age,</u> computers are an essential part of life.

   A. In this day and age,

   B. In this day,

   C. In this age,

   D. Now,

4. <u>In this world in which we live,</u> we need to improve our conservation efforts.

   A. In this world,

   B. In this world we live in,

   C. Now,

   D. In the world today,

5. <u>I was hired and now have</u> a good part-time job.

    A. I was hired and now have

    B. I was hired and have

    C. I now have

    D. I was hired to have

6. He is a <u>brave and courageous</u> person.

    A. brave and courageous

    B. courageous and brave

    C. brave, courageous

    D. courageous

7. You could go shopping <u>during the same time that</u> I'm getting my hair cut.

    A. during the same time that

    B. while

    C. during the time that

    D. at the same time that

8. Be careful, that jellyfish <u>has the ability to</u> sting you.

    A. has the ability to

    B. is able to

    C. can

    D. has ability to

9. Those shoes are <u>brown in color</u> and will match my pants.

    A. brown in color

    B. the color brown

    C. colored brown

    D. brown

10. Remain in your homes <u>until such time as</u> the storm warning has passed.

    A. until such time as

    B. until

    C. until the time that

    D. until the time

Yellow Grammar 17

Subject-Verb Agreement II

Lesson 1: Subject-Verb Disagreement (SVD)

Finding Verbs

The verb is the most important part of a sentence, but verbs aren't always easy to spot. Consider the word *swim* in the sentences *The ducks swim in the pond* and *The ducks love to swim*. In the first sentence, *swim* is the verb. In the second sentence *swim* is not a verb but part of a noun phrase. (*To swim* is the *thing* that the ducks *love*.) So how do we spot verbs?

☐ **A verb is what conveys the essential meaning of a clause** (a string of words that convey an idea). Every idea requires a verb. The sentence *The ducks swim in the pond* says that *Something swims somewhere*, so the verb is *swim*. The sentence *The ducks love to swim* says that *Something loves something*, so the verb is *love*. Every verb requires a **subject**, that is, what *does* the verb. In both sentences, the subject is *ducks*. A verb may also require an *object*, that is, what *receives* the verb. In *The ducks love to swim*, the object is *to swim*, because that is the *thing* that is *loved*.

Spotting a verb can be especially difficult when a sentence is long and has more than one clause. Consider the following:

When David approached third base, the coach waved him home.

This sentence contains two related ideas, so it contains two **clauses**, and therefore two **verbs**:

Clause 1: *When David approached third base*

Verb: *approached*   Subject: *David*   Object: *third base*

Clause 2: *the coach waved him home*

Verb: *waved*   Subject: *the coach*   Object: *him*

Subject-Verb Disagreement

☐ **Every verb must agree in number** (singular or plural) **with its subject. Subject-verb disagreement** is one of the most common errors tested for on the SAT Writing section. The best way to check for subject verb agreement is to find the subject and the verb (ignoring all the intervening words) and **say them together.**
Consider tbis sentence:

The people, who are easily persuaded by corporate sponsored media, spends very little time analyzing issues.

(The verb is *spends* and its subject is *people*. But *people spends* sounds wrong, because *spends* is the "third person singular" –as in *he spends*–but *people* is plural – as in *they spend* - so the phrase should be *people spend*.)

Tricky Plurals and Singulars

These rules will help you to check whether a verb agrees in "number" with its subject:

- [ ] Phrases like *Sam and Bob* are **plural**, but phrases like *Sam, in addition to Bob,* are **singular**. Phrases that start *as well as . . . , together with . . . , along with . . . ,* or *in addition to . . .* are **interrupters**, which are not part of the main subject.

- [ ] These words are **singular**: *each, anyone, anybody, anything, another, neither, either, every, everyone, someone, no one, somebody, everything, little,* and *much*. To check for this SVD, you can replace any of them with *it*.

- [ ] These words are **plural**: *phenomena* (singular: *phenomenon*), *media* (singular: *medium*), *data* (singular: *datum*), and *criteria* (singular: *criterion*). To check for SVD, you can replace any of them with *they*.

- [ ] All of the following can be either **singular or plural**, according to the noun that follows the *of*: *none (of), any (of), some (of), most (of), more (of),* and *all (of)*.

- [ ] Verbs that follow subjects of the form *either A or B* and *neither A nor B* must **agree with** *B*, the noun closer to the verb.

Unauthorized copying or reuse of any part of this page is illegal.

Version 1.3

Inverted Sentences

☐ Usually the subject comes **before** the verb, but **inverted** clauses have the subject **after** the verb. For instance, sentences that start *There is . . .* or *There are . . .* are inverted. To check subject-verb agreement in these sentences, first "uninvert" them.

e.g. *There <u>are</u> many <u>flies</u> in the barn.* (inverted)
       V   S

    Many <u>flies</u> <u>are</u> in the barn. (uninverted)
      S   V

Concept Review 1: Subject-Verb Disagreement

Directions: Next to each noun or noun phrase, write "S" if it is singular or "P" if it is plural.

1. Neither rain nor snow   _____

2. Crowd of rowdy fans   _____

3. Media   _____

4. Criterion   _____

5. One or two   _____

6. Everything   _____

7. Either of the candidates   _____

8. Phenomena   _____

Directions: Circle the subject in each sentence, and choose the correct verb.

9. Neither of the cars (is/are) equipped with anti-lock brakes.

10. The flock of geese (was/were) startled by the shotgun blast.

11. The data on my computer (was/were) completely erased when the power failed.

12. Mathematics and history (is/are) my favorite subjects.

13. None of the roast (was/were) eaten.

14. All of the games (was/were) played on real grass fields.

15. Pride and Prejudice (is/are) my favorite Jane Austen novel.

16. Neither of the twins (is/are) allergic to penicillin.

17. Much of what I hear in those lectures (goes/go) in one ear and out the other.

18. Amy, along with Jamie and Jen, (is/are) applying to Mount Holyoke.

19. None of the books (was/were) considered fit for public consumption.

20. All of the eggplant (was/were) used to make the sauce.

21. Amid the lilies and wildflowers (was/were) one solitary rose.

22. Either Ben or his brothers (is/are) in charge of bringing the drinks.

23. There (is/are) hardly even a speck of dirt left on the carpet.

24. "Stop right there!" (shouts/shout) the Bailey brothers, who are standing in front of me.

25. Either the Donovans or Dave (is/are) going to bring the plates.

26. There (is/are) at least a hundred people here.

Directions: Uninvert the following sentences so that the verb follows the subject, then choose the correct verb form.

27. There (is/are), in my opinion, far too many smokers in this restaurant.

_____

_____

28. Over that hill (is/are) thousands of bison.

_____

_____

29. Riding on the bus among the children (was/were) over a dozen commuters.

_____

_____

30. Never before (has/have) there been such voices heard here.

_____

_____

31. Absent from the article (was/were) any mention of the director's previous Broadway failures.

_____

_____

Worksheet 1: Subject-Verb Disagreement

Directions: Label each verb in the following sentences with a "V" and each subject with an "S." If any verbs are incorrect, cross them out and write the correct form above.

1. We were horrified to discover that there was more than 3 mice living in the attic.

2. Either the president or one of his aides are going to coordinate the project.

3. There is nearly always 2 or 3 guards posted at each entrance.

4. Every player on both the Falcons and the Rockets were at the party after the game.

5. There has been a theater and a toy store in the mall ever since it opened.

6. Either Eric or his brother is hosting the party this year.

7. There is no fewer than 6 crayons in this box.

8. The therapy can resume as planned because neither of the twins are allergic to penicillin.

9. The proceeds from the sale of every auctioned item goes to charity.

10. Economics, particularly with its dependence on the behavior of consumers and producers, has always struck me as more of a human science than a mathematical one.

11. There is more than 3 years remaining on her contract.

12. Neither of the girls were frightened by the wild animals that scurried incessantly past their tent.

13. The technology behind high-definition television, DVDs, and CDs have transformed nearly every aspect of the home entertainment industry.

14. Every player on both teams were concerned about the goalie's injury.

15. The company's sponsorship of charitable foundations and mentorship programs have garnered many commendations from philanthropic organizations.

16. Neither the children nor their parents utters a word when Mrs. Denny tells her stories.

17. How important is your strength training and your diet to your daily regimen?

Lesson 2: Trimming Sentences

Why Trim?

- ☐ Spotting SVD errors is often easier when you "trim" the sentence, that is, eliminate nonessential modifiers to leave the "core" of the sentence. What remains after you "trim" should still be a grammatically correct and complete sentence.

How to "Trim" a Sentence

- ☐ **Step 1: Cross out all nonessential prepositional phrases.**

  e.g. The bird ~~in the cage~~ began singing.

A **preposition** is a word that shows relative position or direction. It can complete one of the following sentences:

The squirrel ran _____ the tree.

Democracy is government _____ the people.

Examples include *to, from, of, for, by, in, before, with, beyond*, and *up*.

A **prepositional phrase** is the preposition and the noun phrase that follows, including its modifiers.

- ☐ **Step 2: Cross out all interrupting phrases.**

  e.g. The committee, ~~ignoring tradition,~~ will approve the measure.

An **interrupting phrase** is a modifying phrase that interrupts the flow of the sentence. Interrupters are generally separated from the main sentence by commas or dashes.

- ☐ **Step 3: Cross out all other nonessential modifiers and modifying phrases.**

  e.g. ~~Having traveled so far,~~ the ~~baseball~~ team hardly wanted to forfeit the ~~championship~~ game.

Modifiers are **adjectives** and **adverbs**, as well as modifying phrases like **participial phrases**. Most modifiers are not essential to a sentence, but some are. Use your best judgment. One kind of essential adjective is a **predicate adjective**, that is, an adjective that is linked to the subject by a linking verb, as in *Martha is <u>smart</u>*.

Trimming a sentence helps you to spot SVD more easily.

Original: *My chief concern with this budget and the other proposals on the table are the cuts in school funds.*

Trimmed: *My concern are the cuts.*

Revised: *My concern <u>is</u> the cuts.*

Who Kicked Whom?

When you write, trim your sentences to play the "Who kicked whom?" exercise. Look at the subject-verb-object ("Who kicked whom?") core, and see if it clearly and forcefully conveys the thought you want to convey.

Original: *The lack of economic programs and no big country's being ready to join it symbolized the problems the League of Nations had in getting established.*

Trimmed: *The lack and no country's being ready symbolized the problems.*

(Yikes! That doesn't make a shred of sense; rewrite it.)

Revised: *Two problems plagued the establishment of the League of Nations: its lack of viable economic programs and its lack of support from the larger countries.*

Concept Review 2: Trimming Sentences

1. What are the three types of words or phrases that can be eliminated when "trimming" a sentence?

    _____

    _____

2. Why is it sometimes helpful to "trim" a sentence?

    _____

    _____

3. Circle all of the prepositions in the list below.

    of   beyond   for   and   with   the   an   without   some   along   below

4. What is a prepositional phrase?

    _____

    _____

5. Write four examples of prepositional phrases.

_____

_____

_____

_____

Directions: Write the trimmed version of each sentence on the line below it, correcting any verb problems.

6. _The team of advisors, arriving ahead of schedule, were met at the airport by the Assistant Prime Minister._

_____

_____

7. _The flock of birds that darted over the lake were suddenly an opalescent silver._

_____

_____

8. _Carmen, along with her 3 sisters, are unlikely to be swayed by arguments supporting David's position._

_____

_____

Directions: Write the trimmed version of each sentence on the line below it, then rewrite the sentence to make it clearer and more forceful, changing the subject and verb entirely, if necessary.

9. *Nearly inevitably, advancements, or those being popularly regarded as such, have to do with modifications, not overhaul.*

Trimmed:

_____

_____

Revised:

_____

_____

10. *The development of the new country's governmental system was affected in a negative regard by the rebels' lack of cohesiveness.*

Trimmed:

_____

_____

Revised:

_____

_____

Worksheet 2: Trimming Sentences

Directions: Write the "trimmed" version of each sentence, circling the verbs and subjects and correcting any agreement errors.

1. *Juggling the demands of both school and my social agenda often seem too much to bear.*

   _____

   _____

2. *Others on the committee, like the chairwoman Amanda Sanders, is concerned about the lack of attention given to school safety.*

   _____

   _____

3. *The waiters' professional demeanor—particularly their keen knowledge, their attention to detail, and their cordiality—are what makes dining there such a sublime culinary experience.*

   _____

   _____

4. *The system by which candidates for local political offices are selected is archaic and, many contend, unfair.*

   _____

   _____

5. *The abundance of companies that fail in their first year of business contribute to an intimidating economic climate.*

   _____

   _____

6. *When scientists theorize about the traits that all humans have come to share, they must be keenly aware of the fact that these traits have evolved over millions of generations.*

   _____

   _____

Unauthorized copying or reuse of any part of this page is illegal.

Version 1.3

7. *The entire industry of tobacco companies and distributors has steadfastly maintained their position that tobacco is not addictive and that smoking is an inalienable right of consumers.*

_____

_____

8. *The challenge of Mount Everest, its conquerors claim, is far more the lack of oxygen at its rarefied heights than even the precarious ice falls or precipitous ascents.*

_____

_____

9. *One in every 3 Americans agree strongly with the statement: "Anyone who would run for political office is not worth voting for."*

_____

_____

10. *The fact that humans have committed so many atrocities have forced some historians to adopt a cynical perspective on human nature.*

_____

_____

Yellow Grammar 18

Mixed Practice

Improving Sentences

Directions: The following sentences test correctness and effectiveness of expression. Part of each sentence or the entire sentence is underlined; beneath each sentence are five ways of phrasing the underlined material. Choice **A** repeats the original phrasing; the other four choices are different. If you think the original phrasing produces a better sentence than any of the alternatives, select choice **A**; if not, select one of the other choices.

1. Laval, the first bishop of Quebec, exemplified aristocratic vigor and concern, <u>on account of his giving up his substantial inheritance to become an ecclesiastic</u> and to help shape Canadian politics and education.

   (A) on account of his giving up his substantial inheritance to become an ecclesiastic

   (B) since he gave up his substantial inheritance to become an ecclesiastic

   (C) since giving up his substantial inheritance to become an ecclesiastic

   (D) because of his having given up his substantial inheritance for the purpose of becoming an ecclesiastic

   (E) as a result of becoming an ecclesiastic through giving up his substantial inheritance

2. Even though the senators on the committee <u>were reluctant to schedule</u> a formal inquiry, they went on record as favoring one.

   (A) were reluctant to schedule

   (B) were reluctant as far as scheduling

   (C) were reluctant in scheduling

   (D) have been reluctant at scheduling

   (E) have had reluctance to schedule

3. Her eyes shining with tears, Aunt Helga told us over and over again how much she appreciated <u>us coming to her</u> ninetieth birthday party.

   (A) us coming to her

   (B) our coming to her

   (C) us having come to her

   (D) that we come to her

   (E) us for the fact of our coming to her

4. Many researchers contend that driving while talking on a cellular phone poses essentially the same risks <u>than if you drive</u> while intoxicated.

   (A) than if you drive

   (B) than to drive

   (C) as if one drives

   (D) as driving

   (E) as it does when driving

5. Before 1988, the corporation's board of directors included one hundred and fifty-three <u>members, none of the members were women</u>.

   (A) members, none of the members were women

   (B) members; and no women

   (C) members, none of them women

   (D) members, and of the members not one of them was a woman

   (E) members; none of them being women

6. <u>The client was waiting for fifteen minutes when</u> the receptionist suddenly looked up from her work, noticed him, and informed him that his appointment had been canceled.

    (A) The client was waiting for fifteen minutes when

    (B) The client, having waited for fifteen minutes, when

    (C) Already the client was waiting for fifteen minutes when

    (D) When the client waited for fifteen minutes,

    (E) The client had been waiting for fifteen minutes when

7. <u>Because the polar ice caps are melting, therefore many</u> scientists and environmentalists fear that several small island nations will be completely covered by water in only a few decades.

    (A) Because the polar ice caps are melting, therefore many

    (B) Because the polar ice caps are melting, many

    (C) The polar ice caps are melting, therefore many

    (D) Because the polar ice caps are melting; many

    (E) The polar ice caps are melting; and many

8. One of the great literary artists of the nineteenth <u>century was Gustave Flaubert known for his obsession with the writer's craft</u>.

    (A) century was Gustave Flaubert known for his obsession with the writer's craft

    (B) century, Gustave Flaubert's obsession with the writer's craft was well known

    (C) century, Gustave Flaubert was known for his obsession with the writer's craft

    (D) century, Gustave Flaubert, known for his obsession with the writer's craft

    (E) century was Gustave Flaubert: known for his obsession with the writer's craft

9. The process by which the community <u>influence the actions of its members</u> is known as social control.

    (A) influence the actions of its members

    (B) influences the actions of its members

    (C) had influenced the actions of its members

    (D) influences the actions of their members

    (E) will influence the actions of its members

10. <u>Play being recognized</u> as an important factor in improving mental and physical health and thereby reducing human misery and poverty.

    (A) Play being recognized as

    (B) By recognizing play as

    (C) Their recognizing play as

    (D) Recognition of it being

    (E) Play is recognized as

Identifying Sentence Errors

Directions: The following sentences test your ability to recognize grammar and usage errors. Each sentence contains either a single error or no error at all. No sentence contains more than one error. The error, if there is one, will be underlined and lettered. If the sentence contains an error, select the letter of the incorrect portion. If the sentence is correct, select choice **E**.

1. We were <u>already</u> <u>to leave for</u> the amusement park when John's car <u>broke down</u>; we <u>were forced</u> to
      A   B   C   D
postpone our outing. <u>No Error</u>
                       E

2. <u>By order of</u> the Student Council, <u>the wearing of</u> slacks by <u>we</u> girls in school <u>has been permitted</u>.
     A   B   C   D
<u>No Error</u>
   E

3. <u>Each</u> one of the dogs in the show <u>require</u> a <u>special</u> <u>kind of</u> diet. <u>No Error</u>
   A   B   C   D   E

4. The major difficulty <u>confronting</u> the authorities <u>was</u> the reluctance of the people <u>to talk</u>; they had
                              A   B   C
been warned not <u>to say nothing</u> to the police. <u>No Error</u>
                  D   E

5. If I <u>were</u> you, I would never permit <u>him</u> <u>to take part</u> in such an <u>exhausting and painful</u> activity.
      A   B   C   D
<u>No Error</u>
  E

6. Stanford White, <u>who</u> is one of America's <u>most notable</u> architects, <u>have designed</u> many famous
                  A   B   C
buildings, <u>among them</u> the original Madison Square Garden. <u>No Error</u>
           D   E

7. The notion <u>of allowing</u> the <u>institution of</u> slavery <u>to continue to</u> exist in a democratic society had no
                A   B   C
appeal to either the violent followers of John Brown <u>nor</u> the peaceful disciples of Sojourner Truth.
                                                          D

<u>No Error</u>
  E

8. Some students <u>prefer</u> watching filmstrips to <u>textbooks</u> because they feel <u>uncomfortable with</u> the
                      A   B   C
presentation <u>of</u> information in a non-oral form. <u>No Error</u>
         D   E

9. <u>There</u> was so much conversation <u>in back of</u> me <u>that</u> I <u>couldn't</u> hear the actors on the stage.
   A   B   C   D
<u>No Error</u>
  E

10. This book is <u>too</u> elementary; <u>it can help</u> neither you <u>nor</u> <u>I</u>. <u>No Error</u>
              A   B   C D   E

Improving Paragraphs Practice

Directions: Read each passage and select the best answers for the questions that follow. Some questions are about particular sentences or parts of sentences and ask you to improve sentence structure or word choice, while other questions ask you to consider organization and development.

Practice Passage 1:

(1) Throughout history, people have speculated about the future. (2) Will it be a utopia? they wondered. (3) Will injustice and poverty be eliminated? (4) Will people accept ethnic diversity, learning to live in peace? (5) Will the world be clean and unpolluted? (6) Or will technology aid us in creating a trap for ourselves we cannot escape, for example such as the world in 1984? (7) With the turn of the millennium just around the corner these questions are in the back of our minds.

(8) Science fiction often portrays the future as a technological Garden of Eden. (9) With interactive computers, TVs and robots at our command, we barely need to lift a finger to go to school, to work, to go shopping, and education is also easy and convenient. (10) Yet, the problems of the real twentieth century seem to point in another direction. (11) The environment, far from improving, keeps deteriorating. (12) Wars and other civil conflicts break out regularly. (13) The world's population is growing out of control. (14) The majority of people on earth live in poverty. (15) Many of them are starving. (16) Illiteracy is a problem in most poor countries. (17) Diseases and malnourishment is very common. (18) Rich countries like the U.S.A. don't have the resources to help the "have-not" countries.

(19) Instead, think instead of all the silly inventions such as tablets that you put in your toilet tank to make the water blue, or electric toothbrushes. (20) More money is spent on space and defense than on education and health care. (21) Advancements in agriculture can produce enough food to feed the whole country, yet people in the U.S. are starving.

(22) Although the USSR is gone, the nuclear threat continues from small countries like Iraq. (23) Until the world puts its priorities straight, we can't look for a bright future in the twenty-first century, despite the rosy picture painted for us by the science fiction writers.

1. Considering the context of paragraph 1, which of the following is the best revision of sentence 6?

   (A) Or will technology create a trap for ourselves from which we cannot escape, for example the world in *1984*?

   (B) Or will technology aid people in creating a trap for themselves that they cannot escape; for example, the world in *1984*?

   (C) Or will technology create a trap from which there is no escape, as it did in the world of *1984*?

   (D) Or will technology trap us in an inescapable world, for example, it did so in the world of *1984*?

   (E) Perhaps technology will aid people in creating a trap for themselves from which they cannot escape, just as they did it in the world of *1984*?

2. With regard to the essay as a whole, which of the following best describes the writer's intention in paragraph 1?

   (A) To announce the purpose of the essay

   (B) To compare two ideas discussed later in the essay

   (C) To take a position on the essay's main issue

   (D) To reveal the organization of the essay

   (E) To raise questions that will be answered in the essay

3. Which of the following is the most effective revision of the underlined segment of sentence 9 below?

   (9) With interactive computers, TVs and robots at our command, we barely need to lift a finger to go to school, to work, <u>to go shopping, and education is also easy and convenient</u>.

   (A) and to go shopping, while education is also easy and convenient

   (B) to go shopping, and getting an education is also easy and convenient

   (C) to go shopping as well as educating ourselves are all easy and convenient

   (D) to shop, and an easy and convenient education

   (E) to shop, and to get an easy and convenient education

4. Which of the following is the most effective way to combine sentences 14, 15, 16, and 17?

   (A) The majority of people on earth are living in poverty and are starving, with illiteracy, and disease and being malnourished are also common problems.

   (B) Common problems for the majority of people on earth are poverty, illiteracy, diseases, malnourishment, and many are illiterate.

   (C) The majority of people on earth are poor, starving, sick, malnourished and illiterate.

   (D) Common among the poor majority on earth is poverty, starvation, disease, malnourishment, and illiteracy.

   (E) The majority of the earth's people living in poverty with starvation, disease, malnourishment and illiteracy as constant threat.

Unauthorized copying or reuse of any part of this page is illegal.

Version 1.3

5. Considering the sentences that precede and follow sentence 19, which of the following is the most effective revision of sentence 19?

   (A) Instead they are devoting resources on silly inventions such as tablets to make toilet tank water blue or electric toothbrushes.

   (B) Instead, they waste their resources on producing silly inventions like electric toothbrushes and tablets for bluing toilet tank water.

   (C) Think of all the silly inventions: tablets you put in your toilet tank to make the water blue and electric toothbrushes.

   (D) Instead, tablets you put in your toilet tank to make the water blue or electric toothbrushes are examples of useless products on the market today.

   (E) Instead of spending on useful things, think of all the silly inventions such as tablets you put in your toilet tank to make the water blue or electric toothbrushes.

6. Which of the following revisions would most improve the overall coherence of the essay?

   (A) Move sentence 7 to paragraph 2

   (B) Move sentence 10 to paragraph 1

   (C) Move sentence 22 to paragraph 2

   (D) Delete sentence 8

   (E) Delete sentence 23

Homework

Identifying Sentence Errors

Read and answer the questions below. On the right-hand side of the paper, write what is wrong with the sentence in your own words.

1. <u>Only</u> recently, the <u>newly</u> organized football as-
   A   B
sociation <u>added</u> two new teams to <u>their</u> league.
         C   D
<u>No Error</u>
   D

2. <u>In view of</u> the controversy with the school
     A
board, neither the teachers <u>nor</u> the principal <u>are</u>
                       B
<u>being</u> considered for promotion <u>at this time</u>.
 C   D
<u>No Error</u>
   E

3. <u>The prospective purchaser</u> of the house left the
          A
premises because he <u>was asked</u> to pay a <u>consider-</u>
               B   C
<u>able higher</u> price <u>than</u> he was able to afford.
              D
<u>No Error</u>
   E

4. While we <u>have rummaged</u> <u>through</u> the attic,
           A   B
we found <u>not only</u> an album of our trip to Europe,
         C
but also a <u>multitude of</u> old news clippings.
          D
<u>No Error</u>
   E

5. Mathematics <u>is</u> not his <u>favorite subject</u>; he
          A   B
finds <u>them</u> <u>too</u> confusing. <u>No Error</u>
   C   D   E

Improving Sentences

Read and answer the questions below. On the right-hand side of the paper, write what is wrong with the original sentence in your own words.

6. Fifty-three thousand shouting <u>enthusiasts filled the stadium, they had come</u> to watch the first game of the season and to cheer the home team.

(A) enthusiasts filled the stadium, they had come

(B) enthusiasts filled the stadium to come

(C) enthusiasts, filling the stadium, had come

(D) enthusiasts filled the stadium; and had come

(E) enthusiasts filling the stadium, who had come

7. During the judging of the animals at the show, the judges could not decide <u>whether Brown's collie or Jones's terrier was the best</u> dog.

(A) whether Brown's collie or Jones's terrier was the best

(B) if Brown's collie of Jones's terrier was the better

(C) whether Brown's collie or Jones's terrier was the better

(D) if Brown's collie of Jones's terrier was the best

(E) whether Brown's collie or Jones's terrier had been the best

8. <u>Finally reviewing the extensive evidence against the defendant</u>, he was found guilty.

(A) Finally reviewing the extensive evidence against the defendant,

(B) Reviewing the extensive evidence against the defendant,

(C) The jury finally reviewed the extensive evidence against the defendant,

(D) When the jury finally reviewed the extensive evidence against the defendant,

(E) The jury finally reviewed the evidence against the defendant,

9. <u>Paul Gauguin was married and had family responsibilities and he</u> ran away to the South Seas to paint.

(A) Paul Gauguin was married and had family responsibilities and he

(B) Although being married and having family responsibilities, Paul Gauguin

(C) Although Paul Gauguin was married and had family responsibilities, he

(D) Being married, and therefore having family responsibilities, Paul Gauguin

(E) Despite the fact that Paul Gauguin was married and had family responsibilities, he

10. A key difference between mice and moles is tail <u>length, a mouse's tail is</u> twice as long as the tail of a mole.

    (A) length, a mouse's tail is

    (B) length; a mouse's tail is

    (C) length, the tail of a mouse is

    (D) length; a mouse's tail, it is

    (E) length, mice's tails are

Improving Paragraphs

Read the short essay below. Use the lines provided to write 5 things that could be done to improve the essay. These things may include combining sentences, moving sentences, deleting sentences, or revising them.

(1) If you are looking for a place of culture and refinement, they are not hard to find. (2) Have you ever considered traveling to cities around the world? (3) There are many beautiful places to visit. (4) Here are some of them.

(5) Paris is known "as the City of Lights." (6) Many people consider this city to be the most beautiful city in the world. (7) The buildings are old and grand, with interesting monuments such as the Arc de Triomphe and the Eiffel Tower. (8) Paris is also a home of fashion and cuisine. (9) Not only are there beautiful sights, but you can find also great clothes and great food too! (10) Paris was often threatened by the armies of other countries.

(11) Maybe Europe isn't your dream destination. (12) There are plenty of other places around the world. (13) How about a trip to one of the most high-techest cities in the world, Tokyo? (14) This metropolis is home to wonders both older and newer. (15) For example, you can visit the Emperor's Palace and several shrines that are hundreds of years old. (16) In the same city you can see some of the world's most advanced technology. (17) Tokyo truly is a city of contrasts.

(18) One doesn't need to leave the United States to have a vacation that you will remember for the rest of your life. (19) Why not New York? (20) An important city, New York has much to recommend it. (21) There are many museums to visit. (22) Historical sites, too. (23) If you want to spend time outside, visit Central Park. (24) Catch a show on Broadway if you want some culture.

(25) All three of these cities are examples of great cities in the world. (26) Each have something to recommend them.

1. _____

_____

_____

2. _____

_____

_____

3.

4.

5.

Yellow Writing 19

Pronouns II

Lesson 1: Pronoun-Antecedent Disagreement

Pronouns

A **pronoun** is a word (such as *it, he, she, what,* or *that*) that substitutes for a noun. A pronoun is either **definite** (*it, you, she, I*) and refers to a specified thing (or person or place or idea) or **indefinite** (*anyone, neither, those*), and does **not** refer to a specific thing (or person or place or idea).

Definite Pronouns and Antecedents

☐ Every definite pronoun refers to a noun called an **antecedent.** The pronoun **must agree in number** (singular or plural) **and kind** (personal or impersonal) with the antecedent.

Wrong: *Everyone should brush their teeth 3 times a day.*
             (Because *everyone* is singular, *their* is the wrong pronoun.)

Right: *Everyone should brush his or her teeth 3 times a day.*

Wrong: *David was the one that first spotted the error.*
             (The pronoun *that* is impersonal, but of course, *David* is a person.)

Right: *David was the one who first spotted the error.*

☐ The antecedent of a definite pronoun should be clear, not ambiguous.

Wrong: *Roger told Mike that he was going to start the next game.*
             (Who was going to start? Roger or Mike?)

Right: *Mike learned that he was going to start the next game when Roger told him so.*